TWAYNE'S WORLD AUTHORS SERIES
A Survey of the World's Literature

Sylvia E. Bowman, Indiana University

GENERAL EDITOR

FRANCE

Maxwell A. Smith, Guerry Professor of French, Emeritus
The University of Chattanooga
Former Visiting Professor in Modern Languages
The Florida State University

EDITOR

Beaumarchais

TWAS 334

Beaumarchais

Beaumarchais

By Joseph Sungolowsky

*Queens College of the City University
of New York*

Twayne Publishers, Inc.   ::   New York

Library of Congress Cataloging in Publication Data

Sungolowsky, Joseph.
  Beaumarchais.

  (Twayne's world authors series, TWAS 334. France)
  Bibliography: p. 109.
  1. Beaumarchais, Pierre Augustin Caron de, 1732-1799.
PQ1956.S8   842'.5   74-10580
ISBN 0-8057-2122-3

For Honey and Robert Yves

Contents

About the Author

Joseph Sungolowsky is associate professor of French Literature at Queens College of the City University of New York. He was educated at the Lycée de Nice (France) where he received the Baccalauréat-ès-Lettres. He holds a B.A. degree from Yeshiva University, an M.A. from New York University and a Ph.D. from Yale University. Before coming to Queens, he taught at Yale and Vassar College. Dr. Sungolowsky is the author of *Alfred de Vigny et le dix-huitième siècle* (Paris: Nizet, 1968), and has contributed articles and reviews to various scholarly journals.

Preface

Throughout the years, the figure of Beaumarchais has retained the attention of many biographers, historians, and critics. The extraordinary career of the commoner who, at first, imperiled the Parlement under Louis XV and, later, narrowly escaped the guillotine of the French Revolution represents a fertile subject for those who choose to follow in detail the evolution of his adventures. Mindful of the intricacies of nearly every phase of his life, some have gone as far as scrutinizing a precise episode such as his role of secret agent or defender of American independence. Various conclusions are drawn leaving the image of a controversial Beaumarchais suspicious to some and congenial to others. It is evident, however, that he did not think of himself as merely playing with destiny. He felt, rather, deeply involved in a life experience worthy of universal expression. This is why most of those who studied Beaumarchais the man agreed to see in him the father of his immortal creation, Figaro.

Neither does Beaumarchais the author lack commentators. The early studies of Loménie and Lintilhac have done ample justice to his work, stressing the merits of that which was to be retained by posterity. Many critics have subsequently approached Beaumarchais in a lighter fashion stating that he deserves to be known chiefly for his *Mémoires* against Goezman, his *Barbier de Séville*, and *Mariage de Figaro*. While it is true that much of Beaumarchais's prose and dramatic production is forgotten, such an evaluation is somewhat hasty.

This study primarily considers Beaumarchais as an author. In the opening chapter, I have presented a short biographical account that tries, as often as possible, to allow Beaumarchais himself to comment, sometimes with an amusing fantasy, on the events of his life. The *Mémoires* against Goezman undoubtedly represent a masterpiece of polemical literature. Yet, I have attempted to show that the devices Beaumarchais used so successfully in these writings are not totally lacking from his later polemics where his arguments are still convincing.

I have dwelt on the prefaces Beaumarchais wrote for his plays because they present the various attitudes he assumed as a man of the theater. In his first manifesto, he appears as the long-awaited champion of the *drame* which must overshadow the now irrelevant classical theater. When his *Barbier de Séville* proved to be a success, he allowed himself to jeer wittingly at those who had wished to destroy it. Aware of the subtle subversiveness of his *Mariage de Figaro,* he asserted convincingly that he had merely intended to write a morality play.

I have dealt at some length with the dramas. While recognizing the weaknesses for which they are usually known, I have pointed to their structure which already shows that Beaumarchais was concerned with building a solid intrigue. Although *La Mère coupable* is a sequel to the comedies and *Tarare* is an opera, I have included them in the chapter on the drama for their themes belong to the sensibility genre.

Although Beaumarchais always asserted that he made his debut in the theater with his dramas, I have examined his *Parades* so as to show the comic resources on which they are based. I have followed the transformation of *Le Barbier de Séville* from what may have been a parade into a full-fledged comedy and analyzed it so as to bring out the underlying mechanism of its complex intrigue. Since Beaumarchais has multiplied intrigue, created more complex characters, and considerably extended the function of comedy in *Le Mariage de Figaro,* I have devoted to it the final chapter.

Translations are my own. For the two comedies, I have availed myself of those by Brobury Pearce Ellis, which I found both elegant and accurate.

JOSEPH SUNGOLOWSKY

Queens College of the
City University of New York

Acknowledgment

My thanks are hereby expressed to AHM Publishing Corporation for permission to quote from *The Barber of Seville* and *The Marriage of Figaro,* edited and translated by Brobury Pearce Ellis, New York: Appleton-Century-Crofts, 1966.

J. S.

Chronology

1732   Pierre-Augustin Caron is born in Paris, January 24.

1753   Author of a *mémoire* addressed to the Academy of Sciences against the watchmaker Lepaute who claims the invention of a mechanism for watches originally devised by Pierre-Augustin Caron.

1754   The Academy declares young Caron's claim justified.

1755   Beginnings at the court of Louis XV.

1756   Marries the widow of Franquet, a Clerk Controller at the Court. She dies ten months later.

1757   Adopts the name Beaumarchais.
        Enters the milieu of Charles Lenormand d'Etioles.
        Composes the *Parades*. Meets Pâris-Duverney.

1761   Becomes a nobleman and buys the office of "Lieutenant-général de la Varenne du Louvre."

1764–

1766   Stay in Spain. Clavijo affair.

1767   *Eugénie* is presented at the Comédie-Française, January 29.

1768   Marries the widow of Lévêque, a Court official.
        She dies two years later.

1770   *Les Deux Amis* is presented at the Comédie-Française, January 13. Pâris-Duverney dies, July 15.

1773   Quarrel with the Duc de Chaulnes (February 11) followed by Beaumarchais's incarceration at the For-Lévêque.

1774   Goezman Affair. Condemned to *blâme*. Accomplishes missions abroad.

1775   *Le Barbier de Séville* is presented at the Comédie-Française, February 23. Continues his activities as a secret agent. Becomes interested in the cause of American independence.

1776   The *blâme* is lifted. Supplies weapons to the American insurgents.

1777   Undertakes to defend the rights of authors against the actors of the Comédie-Française.

1784   *Le Mariage de Figaro* is presented at the Comédie-Française, April 21.

1785   Establishes the Compagnie des Eaux de Paris.

1786   Marries Marie-Thérèse Willermaulaz who had been his mistress for ten years and bore him a daughter.

1787   *Tarare* is presented at the Opera. Kornman affair.

1790   Completes the publication of Voltaire's works at Kehl. Second presentation of *Tarare* with a new ending adapted to the political climate of the French Revolution.

1792   *La Mère coupable* is presented at the Théâtre du Marais, June 26. The guns affair. Publication of the *Mémoires des Six Epoques*. Lives in exile.

1796   Returns to France.

1799   Dies, May 18.

CHAPTER 1

An Embattled Writer

T HE life of Beaumarchais is a subject in itself and many
biographies have unfolded to various extent its colorful
intricacies and details. Yet, one cannot claim to analyze his work
without constant reference to his life, for in Beaumarchais's case the
former is an outgrowth of the latter. For better or for worse,
Beaumarchais wrote effusively in nearly all the circumstances of his
multifaceted career. Although he achieved literary fame in self-
defence or as an author of comedies, his writings concerning his
adventures as a secret agent or his fabulous business enterprises
often deserve consideration, as they illustrate how reality stimulated
his imagination. Thus, the sketch of Beaumarchais's life presented
here points to the existence of a kind of autobiography that is also a
part of his work.

I *The Advocate of Justice*

At the age of eighteen, young Pierre-Augustin Caron was ban-
ished from his father's watchmaker's shop, as he failed to show himself
a dutiful apprentice. While inwardly resenting such harsh punish-
ment incurred for youthful escapades, he quickly declared his
readiness to adhere to the strict behavior his father imposed upon
him as a condition for forgiveness. The young man must have
realized that the impulsiveness of adolescence was no excuse for in-
temperate waywardness, as he wrote to his father: ". . . it is right
that I suffer the humiliation I have justly deserved, and if all this,
added to my good conduct, can procure for me and merit entirely
the return of your good graces and friendship, I shall only be too
happy."[1] Three years later, Pierre-Augustin was seeking justice for
himself, as a friend of the family, the watchmaker Lepaute, claimed
to be the inventor of a simplified escapement system for watches he
had devised. He denounced the fraud in a *mémoire* addressed to the

Academy of Sciences which already reveals the style of his future in-
dictments of Goezman. He asks the Academy not to discredit his invention because of his youth. He explains that, seeking to perfect the
art of watchmaking under the guidance of his father, he often shared
his findings with Lepaute but soon realized that he was being
deceived. In his endeavor to convince the Academy that Lepaute's
invention is really his own, he writes: "Let him prove, as I do, the
succession of his ideas, the gradual chain of successes which lead to
the desired end; let him prove it by similar unsuspicious witnesses,
and there will remain no doubt as to the author of the discovery."[2]

The Academy recognized the legitimacy of young Caron's
grievance as well as his craftsmanship. He was appointed the Court's
watchmaker, and the ambitious young commoner could thus mingle
with the nobility. Madeleine-Catherine Franquet, née Aubertin,
wife of a Clerk Controller at the Court, soon showed interest in him
although she was older than he by ten years. Following the death of
her husband, Pierre-Augustin married her and acquired the Court
office of the deceased. Among the assets of his wife was the village of
Beaumarchais, a name he added to his own. After ten months of
marriage, his wife died. In 1768, he married Geneviève-Madeleine
Lévêque, the wealthy widow of a court official, who died two years
later. The son she bore him died at the age of three. Beaumarchais's
enemies deliberately cast suspicion on those short-lived marriages by
spreading the rumors that he had poisoned his wives in order to inherit their wealth. Beaumarchais bitterly denounced the baseness of
such accusations. Replying to them, he wrote later: "As for my
wives, I had two and not three as the perfidious gazeteer contends.
Failing to register my marriage contract, the death of my first wife
left me naked, in the fullest sense of the word . . . overpowered by
debts. . . . My second wife, at her death, has taken with her more
than three quarters of her fortune . . . so that my son, had he lived,
would have been richer by far through his father than through his
mother."[3] Indeed, in the suit brought against Beaumarchais by the
heirs of Mme Franquet, he was declared their creditor, and his
touching devotion to the former Mme Lévêque is known by the fact
that he held her embraced on her deathbed against the advice of the
well-known physician Tronchin.[4]

At the court of Louis XV, Beaumarchais gained influential allies.
Among them were none other than the daughters of the king who

were delighted by his skillful playing of the harp. He soon offered to give them music lessons. Such a meteoric rise excited the jealousy of less fortunate noblemen. One of them shrewdly resolved to remind him of his former trade by asking him to examine the quality of his watch. Beaumarchais informed him that having ceased to practice long ago, he had become very clumsy. Feigning to examine the watch, he picked it up and dropped it to the amusement of the bystanders. His friendship with Charles Lenormand d'Etioles, the husband of Madame de Pompadour, gave him the opportunity to meet the financier Pâris-Duverney with whom he began a successful business association. Beaumarchais became a rich man and was able to purchase the title of Secretary of the King as well as the office of Lieutenant-General of Hunting of La Varenne du Louvre.

Yet, Beaumarchais never concealed his origins. When rumors spread that he was ashamed of his father, he hurried to introduce him to the princesses. In his *Mémoires*, he takes pride time and again to assert the close relationship he had always maintained with his family. He writes about his enemies: "Those wretched people say that my life is a pack of horrors while it is known that I have spent it being the father and the support of whoever is close to me. They speak so much evil of me that I am forced to praise myself" (522). According to Beaumarchais, it was at his father's behest that he suddenly left the Court and traveled to Spain in 1764 in order to seek justice from Don José Clavijo y Fajardo, archivist of the king and editor of the prestigious review *El Pensador*, who had broken his engagement to Beaumarchais's sister Marie-Louise, or Lisette, Caron. On several occasions, Beaumarchais frightened Clavijo who rescinded his decision and repeatedly promised to marry Lisette. When Clavijo failed to keep his promise in the end, Beaumarchais unmasked him in high places, and he lost his office. Despite the unhappy outcome, justice was done and Lisette's honor was safe. According to René Pomeau, the Clavijo episode, as Beaumarchais describes it in the fourth *Mémoire* against Goezman, is not only a drama in itself but echoes his first drama *Eugénie* where a brother also flies to rescue the honor of his sister.[5]

In truth, Beaumarchais's trip to Spain did not have as unselfish motives as he would have us believe. On the one hand, Lisette's past life in Madrid had not been beyond reproach. On the other, Beaumarchais had been asked by Pâris-Duverney to negotiate with the Spanish government an authorization for his men to pursue the slave trade in Louisiana that the French had just surrendered to Spain. Beaumarchais was no more successful in this enterprise than in the Clavijo affair. However, these failures did not keep him from leading a gay life which gave him the opportunity to observe the mores of the Spanish people. In his letter of December 24, 1764, addressed to the Duc de la Vallière, Beaumarchais writes of the excessive spendings of noblemen, the abuses of the government, the severity of censorship, the orgiastic character of life in Madrid, and the obscenity of the *fandango*, a popular dance among the Spaniards that Beaumarchais describes in detail.[6]

Beaumarchais dreaded the approaching death of Pâris-Duverney who had designated as his heir to a fortune of one and a half million francs[7] a grandnephew, Count Falcoz de la Blache. The latter had deliberately looked with suspicion at Beaumarchais's dealings with his granduncle and had publicly declared that he hated Beaumarchais "as much as a lover loves his mistress." Although La Blache was carefully watching the last days of the dying financier, Beaumarchais succeeded in arranging with his associate clandestine meetings in order to settle their respective accounts. On April 1, 1770, a balance sheet was drawn up in which Pâris-Duverney declared himself Beaumarchais's debtor for 15,000 francs and committed himself to lend him 75,000 francs without interest over a period of eight years. Pâris-Duverney died in July of the same year without executing the clauses of his settlement with Beaumarchais. On taking possession of his inheritance, La Blache declared the balance sheet a forgery asserting that Beaumarchais had drawn it up himself on one of the signed blank forms Pâris-Duverney used to leave behind. According to La Blache's calculations, Beaumarchais had been Pâris-Duverney's debtor for 139,000 francs. The matter was debated in court which ruled in favor of Beaumarchais. La Blache appealed the decision to the hightest judicial authority, the Parlement.

In December, 1770, Chancellor Maupeou formed a new Parlement which he strongly controlled to the extent that the king himself was intimidated by it. On April 1, 1773, four days before the judgment on the litigation between Beaumarchais and La Blache, Councillor Louis-Valentin Goezman, a protégé of Maupeou, was appointed to report on the case. La Blache had apparently succeeded in gaining the favors of Goezman, whose reputation for corruption was well known. Beaumarchais was unable to act as quickly as his opponent since he was detained in prison following his altercation with the Duc de Chaulnes, who was brutalizing his mistress who had sought Beaumarchais's protection. Nevertheless, Beaumarchais was allowed to visit Goezman under guard in order to enlighten him on his case. Goezman refused to see Beaumarchais unless he received the sum of a hundred louis, as it was relayed to Beaumarchais through Madame Goezman. Beaumarchais complied but realized the councillor's partiality in the course of his brief interview with him. Beaumarchais sought, therefore, to see him again and learned from Madame Goezman that she could arrange another interview at the cost of an additional hundred louis plus fifteen louis for her husband's secretary. Unable to obtain the cash, Beaumarchais presented her with a diamond clock valued at one hundred louis to which he added the fifteen louis she had requested. In his first mémoire against Goezman, Beaumarchais amusingly itemized the ten attempts he made to see the councillor between April 1 and 5, which resulted in a single interview granted. As could be expected, the Parlement, acting on Goezman's recommendation, ruled against Beaumarchais. In a letter he wrote to the king, Beaumarchais describes the misfortunes that befell him as a result of the unfair judgment, namely the expulsion of his family from his house, the seizure of his possessions, and his failing health due to the unsanitary conditions of the prison to which he had been sent for reasons unknown to him. [8]

Following the unfavorable outcome, Madame Goezman returned the hundred louis and the clock but not the fifteen louis claiming that the secretary had kept them. Suspecting Madame Goezman of concealing the truth, Beaumarchais, with the facetiousness that he handles so well, wrote to her: "I have been so horribly mistreated in the report of your husband, and my defenses have been so much trampled by the one who, according to you, was to give them a legitimate attention, that it is unfair to add to the enormous losses this report costs me that of fifteen golden louis which cannot have been mislaid in your hands. If injustice is to be repaid, it cannot be by him who suffers so cruelly from it." [9] Goezman could not possibly have his wife return the fifteen louis without jeopardizing his position. In order to silence Beaumarchais, he accused him of attempt—

ing to corrupt a judge. Fearing an adverse verdict, especially in view of the pamphlets written against him by Goezman and his friends, Beaumarchais decided to bring his case before the public. He gathered a staff composed of his father, his sisters, his brothers-in-law, and several friends, who advised him on the composition of the five mémoires against Goezman written between September, 1773, and February, 1774, that were immediately hailed as a masterpiece of polemics in France and all over Europe.

The Parlement had no other choice but to dismiss Goezman from office while imposing the infamous sentence of *blâme* on Madame Goezman as well as on Beaumarchais and condemning his mémoires to be burned. Despite the severity of the verdict, Beaumarchais had won an uncontested victory, and, as Louis de Loménie writes, it was his lot "to kindle, by a suit of fifteen louis, the flame that was to destroy Maupeou and his Parlement."[10] Indeed, as soon as Louis XVI acceded to the throne in the same year, he dissolved the Parlement and restored the former one. Having served the new king for two years and strengthened his credit at the Court, Beaumarchais requested the Parlement to reexamine his case. In an address he intended to pronounce before the Tribunal, he evoked his struggle against the former Parlement in these words: "Gentlemen, let us forget the past. Restore me to my former status as a citizen. I shall believe, then, that I am awakening from a horrible dream in which I see myself wandering painfully in the night for a long time, pursued by ghosts" (362). Beaumarchais was excused from speaking on his own behalf, for his lawyers had successfully pleaded his case and won his rehabilitation. However, it was not until July, 1778, that he finally triumphed over La Blache before the Parlement of Aix-en-Provence, after he had written three mémoires against him.

It was in the cause of justice that Beaumarchais decided to become involved in the Kornman affair in 1781. At the age of fifteen, Madame Kornman had been married against her will to Guillaume Kornman, an Alsatian banker, and had brought him a dowry of 360,000 francs. As the marriage was not faring well, she became the mistress of Daudet de Jossan. Kornman feigned to disregard his wife's liaison since Daudet had introduced him to the Prince de Montbarey, the Minister of War, who procured for Kornman lucrative business. But when Montbarey was dismissed from office and when Madame Kornman refused to hand over her dowry,

Kornman accused her of adultery and had her imprisoned, although she was pregnant with her third child. When the Prince of Nassau-Siegen and his wife tried to get their friend Beaumarchais interested in the fate of this woman unknown to him, he showed some reluctance, explaining to them that the defense of justice had always brought him much annoyance. Yet, on hearing the plea Madame Kornman addressed to the Court, he declared: "this cannot be the work of an evil woman, and the husband who torments her is either very much mistaken about her or very wicked himself." Upon reading the correspondence between Kornman and Daudet which showed clearly that their friendship lasted only as long as Daudet proved himself useful, Beaumarchais had a sudden change of heart. Describing this moment, he writes: "I went to a terrace where I read them [the letters] eagerly. Blood rushed to my head. When I finished, I entered and said with passion: "You can dispose of me, and I am ready to accompany you, princess, to M. Le Noir the lieutenant of police in order to plead eagerly the cause of an unfortunate woman who is being punished for the crime of someone else' " (458). Beaumarchais succeeded in having Madame Kornman transferred to an accoucheur's house. Nevertheless, in 1789, a few months before the Revolution, he had to contend with the pamphlets of Bergasse, an able lawyer engaged by Kornman, who denounced Beaumarchais as a depraved man representing the crumbling political regime. Beaumarchais replied with three mémoires exposing Kornman's machinations. The latter and Bergasse were condemned for slander. However, Beaumarchais's celebrity had declined a great deal in the eyes of the public which was rather sympathetic to Bergasse. According to Pomeau, Bergasse's charge concerning a liaison between Beaumarchais and Madame Kornman is not totally unfounded.[11]

II *The Secret Agent*

Despite his moral victory over Goezman, Beaumarchais remained a *blâmé,* a legal status which stripped him of his civil rights. Louis XV offered him an opportunity to redeem himself, when he entrusted him with a secret mission. Beaumarchais was to negotiate with Théveneau de Morande, a French adventurer and blackmailer living in London, who threatened to publish a scandalous pamphlet concerning Madame Du Barry, the king's mistress. Under the anagrammatic name of Monsieur de Ronac, Beaumarchais enthusiastically undertook the task. He was soon able to report to the king that he had arranged with Théveneau de Morande for three thousand copies of the pamphlet to be burned, and, moreover, had convinced him to become "a watchful spy for France."[12] Unfortunately, Louis XV died without reinstating Beaumarchais.

Once engaged upon a career as a secret agent, Beaumarchais seems to have developed a taste for it. He informed Louis XVI, the new king, that a Jew named Angelucci alias Atkinson was prepared to publish in London and Amsterdam a libel slandering the royal couple on the sterility of their marriage. Through M. de Sartines, the lieutenant of police, Beaumarchais besought the king to empower him to negotiate with Angelucci. He wrote to Sartines: "No one can assure him [the king] as well as you that the name of His Majesty which is sacred to me will never be jeopardized in any way. I shall regard it as the Israelites regarded the name of Yaweh of which they pronounced the syllables only in the case of supreme necessity."[13] Beaumarchais soon obtained from the king a written authorization, which he enclosed in a golden box and hung around his neck on a gold chain.

In his correspondence, Beaumarchais has given a detailed account of this mission which possesses all the qualities of a thrilling narrative. Having agreed not to publish the libel in London, Angelucci made his way to Holland, where he renewed his threats. Beaumarchais pursued him but learned on arrival that his man had fled to Nuremberg. In a letter written to a friend on August 15, 1774, while crossing the Danube in a boat on his way to Vienna, Beaumarchais tells how he was attacked by bandits in the Lichtenholtz forest at Neustadt near Nuremberg. He was traveling in a post chaise when he decided to get off for a while and ordered the coachman to drive on and wait for him at the outskirts of the forest. Suddenly, a man brandishing a long knife stood in his way. Beaumarchais seized his pistol and kept his foe in check while returning to the coach. He was soon overtaken by someone from behind. In a split second, he decided that in order to deal with the second bandit he must rid himself of the first. At that moment, his pistol misfired. Before he could seize the second bandit, he was thrown to the ground by the first, who struck him with his knife. Luckily, the blade hit the golden box containing the king's authorization and only slightly scratched his chest but inflicted a more serious cut under his chin. "Had I lost my head in this extreme danger," writes Beaumarchais, "it is certain that I would have also lost my life. Rising up with strength, I said to myself '*I am not dead.*' "[14] He struggled with his assailant, threw him to the ground, and succeeded in taking away his knife, deeply cutting his own hand in the process. Upon realizing his disadvantage, the second bandit fled but soon returned with "a few more rascals of his kind." Beaumarchais, who had overcome the first bandit, was once again in danger. The coachman, who was worried by Beaumarchais's prolonged absence, arrived on the scene sounding his horn, thus driving away the bandits. Beaumarchais drew the following portrait of himself after this adventure: "My business is finished, but I look like a mask with my gash, my bandages, my swollen and wrapped up arm. Add to this that I wince like a tortured man each time I breathe so that I make about forty faces per minute."[15] Retelling the event in a letter written to his friend Gudin a day later, Beaumarchais is less dramatic and more philosophical about the matter. He claims that he was ready to die with the thought that his life up to that point had been well spent.

To the officials at Nuremberg, Beaumarchais declared that the bandit he had defeated called the other Atkinson. His duty was, therefore, to proceed to Vienna and warn Marie-Thérèse, the empress of Austria and the mother of Marie-Antoinette, the Queen of France, that Angelucci-Atkinson is to be sought out in order to halt the publication of the libel. Beaumarchais was received by Marie-Thérèse. He showed her a copy of the libel and suggested to her that an expurgated copy of it be published so that it may be shown to Louis XVI. Prince Von Kaunitz, chancellor of Austria, never found the bandits. He suspected Beaumarchais to be a mere adventurer, even himself the author of the libel, and had him put under house arrest. On returning to Paris in October, 1774, Beaumarchais expressed his indignation over his treatment in Vienna. Reporting to the king, he writes: "Everything is taken away from me, knife, scissors, even my buckles, and these numerous guards are left in my room where they stayed thirty-one days or forty-four thousand and six hundred and forty minutes, for, while the happy people barely realize that the hours run so fast, the unfortunate ones split the duration of grief into minutes and seconds that appear to them quite long."[16]

It is most unlikely that Beaumarchais was the author of the pamphlet, as Von Kaunitz maintained. Sartines believed that Beaumarchais was light-headed but not dishonest. Furthermore, he would not have darkened his reputation in view of his existing *blâme* and in the face of his enemies. It is otherwise, however, with the story of the Lichtenholtz forest. According to the testimony of the coachman, Beaumarchais had, indeed, left the coach, but he had taken along his razor. When he returned with cuts on his face and his hand wrapped in a handkerchief, he declared that he had been attacked by bandits. The coachman rather believed that Beaumarchais had inflicted upon himself these wounds that did not appear to be very serious. In all probability, Beaumarchais made up this amusing comedy in which Figaro's razor played an important role, as Lintilhac says.[17] Pomeau thinks that the episode does not lack dramatic perfection, and, as usual, Beaumarchais plays the part of the noble hero.[18]

In May, 1775, Beaumarchais was sent once again to London to negotiate with the Chevalier d'Eon, a former ambassador under Louis XV, who held in his possession a secret correspondence of the late king which he was willing to sell for the enormous sum of three hundred thousand livres. Moreover, the Chevalier, whose sex was subject to speculation, had chosen to live as a woman, and Louis XVI wanted him to go on living as such. Although the autopsy subsequently revealed that he was a perfectly normal man, the king, Vergennes—the minister of foreign affairs—and Beaumarchais himself were convinced that he was a woman. He wrote to Louis XVI: "When one thinks that this creature who has been persecuted so much belongs to the sex that is forgiven for everything, the heart is filled with gentle compassion."[19] Trusting his ability to deal with women, Beaumarchais assured the king that his mission would soon reach a successful ending. He even believed that d'Eon was in love with him. "Everybody tells me," he wrote to Vergennes, "that this foolish woman is madly in love with me. She thinks that I despise her, and women do not forgive such an offense. I am far from despising her. . . . I find this adventure so funny that it is difficult for me to remain serious in order to finish this report correctly."[20] Beaumarchais knew how to make the most of his mission. He explained to Vergennes that it was far easier for an ambassador to conduct an open negotiation than for a secret agent to handle a mysterious affair. Nonetheless, Beaumarchais added concrete achievements to this self-praise, for the secret correspondence had been handed over to him. When he submitted to the king an itemized account of his mission in England and requested him to write an appreciation on his handling of the d'Eon affair, Louis XVI, indeed, wrote on the same report "Bon."[21]

III *The American Enterprise*

During his stays in England, Beaumarchais often visited Lord Rochford, the minister of foreign affairs, whom he had met in Spain, and Wilkes, the mayor of London. These influential leaders of the opposition to the government provided him with firsthand information on the conflict between England and her American colonies. As a disciple of the Enlightenment, Beaumarchais immediately took to heart the cause of the American insurgents and became convinced that France must help them with equipment, weapons, and ammunition. As he later wrote to Vergennes, he also saw an opportunity to take revenge on England for imposing the shameful treaty of 1762 upon the French at the close of the Seven Years' war. However, Louis XVI was reluctant to step into a conflict that had no apparent bearing on the interests of France. In four mémoires addressed to the king between September, 1775, and February, 1776, Beaumarchais undertook to prove why it was essential for France to intervene. According to Beaumarchais, many people in England thought that the colonies were definitely lost. The French sugar islands were in danger of being seized by the English who wanted to eliminate the trade between those islands and the American colonies. Beaumarchais further asserted that, in case of defeat, the Americans would probably join the English in seizing those territories. Arthur Lee, the delegate of Congress in London, had assured him that France would receive Virginian tobacco in exchange for her help. Finally, Beaumarchais was convinced that France could remain at peace only by supporting the rift between England and her colonies. Should France hesitate to act directly, he was willing to establish a firm which would handle the task with the unofficial backing of the government.

It should be noted that Beaumarchais was motivated more by his vivid emotionalism, his passions for political intrigues, or his taste for complicated business deals than by the reality of the situation. Brian

Morton observes that it was not until the surrender of the English at Saratoga in October, 1777, that public opinion in England became uncertain about victory.[22] Bernard Fay points out that the defeated Americans would not have been in any position to fight alongside the English in order to seize the sugar islands. Arthur Lee was by no means empowered to offer France a treaty of commerce, and, in fact, was lying. Yet Beaumarchais reiterated these arguments in his mémoires to Versailles without looking into their validity.[23] Indeed, France adopted his suggestions and lent him a million francs toward the establishment of his firm. With another million lent by Spain who feared for her own sugar islands, Beaumarchais was able to become the founder of the firm Roderigue Hortalez & Co.

Beaumarchais's enterprise met with many hindrances. At the outset, the French government, which wanted to avoid a confrontation with England, held up the departure of his ships. A certain Dubourg, who wanted to supply the Americans on his own, resolved to discredit him in the eyes of Vergennes by writing that he was keeping women. Beaumarchais sarcastically replied that the kept women were none other than his sisters and a niece who had always counted on his support. Above all, he had to contend with American ingratitude. In August, 1776, he assured the deputies of Congress that in exchange for ten or twelve thousand barrels of "Virginian tobacco of the best quality," he would try to eliminate all political obstacles that lay in the way of American endeavors in Europe as well as in France. He wrote: "I dare promise you, gentlemen, that my indefatigable zeal will forget nothing in order to clear difficulties, smooth prohibitions, and facilitate all the operations of a trade that I have undertaken much less for my advantage than for yours."[24] The Americans hardly sent anything, especially since Arthur Lee, who had become Beaumarchais's enemy, convinced Congress that all his shipments were a gift from France. Nevertheless, Beaumarchais's devotion to the cause of American independence did not weaken. In December, 1777, he wrote to De Francy, his agent in America: "Amid all this annoyance, the news from America fills me with joy. Brave, brave people whose military conduct justifies my esteem and the fine enthusiasm it generates in France. Finally, my friend, I want returns only to be able to serve them anew, to meet my commitments so that I may make others in their favor."[25] In 1793, Alexander Hamilton acknowledged that

Beaumarchais was America's creditor for over two million francs. Two years later, fearing that the debt would never be paid, Beaumarchais addressed to the Congress an impassioned plea asking that his daughter be adopted as a child of the State after his death. Should the Congress still refuse to pay, he was ready to travel to America despite his old age and failing health and have himself carried on a stretcher into the national assemblies to ask for charity in return for his accumulated services.[26]

In 1779, when Lord Stormont, the English ambassador at Versailles, qualified the French attitude as "perfidious" and reproached Beaumarchais for helping the Americans, he replied in a pamphlet entitled *Observations sur le mémoire justificatif de la cour de Londres*, in which he defended France's role and his own. Indeed, to have witnessed American independence was one of the great satisfactions of Beaumarchais's life. In one of his last letters, he wrote: ". . . among my great works, I claim with pride to have contributed more than any other European to make America free, to tear her away from her English oppressors. . . ."[27] And, as Loménie observes, France's ultimate recognition of the United States is definitely the work of Beaumarchais.[28]

IV *A Tormented Businessman*

Beaumarchais was not unaware of the commercial aspect of Literature, and he did not hesitate to become entangled in litigations and struggles when he thought that his interests were at stake. Amid the storm of the American enterprise, he set out to obtain just legislation that would defend the rights of authors against the actors of the Comédie-Française. Authors were indeed discouraged from writing for the Comédie-Française, which claimed nine-tenths of the proceeds that were often drawn up arbitrarily. Furthermore, the actors would often declare a play unsuccessful and subsequently present it as their property, with no obligations to the author. In 1775, when the *Barbier de Séville* proved to be a success at the box office, Beaumarchais demanded an itemized statement of accounts. Knowing his reputation for polemics, the actors sought to settle with him on several occasions. Beaumarchais refused, however, explaining that he was not seeking his own interest but rather that of his colleagues. In 1777, he founded the *Société des auteurs dramatiques*, which was to present a united front against the

actors. Disunity among the authors and the craftiness of the actors'
lawyer greatly hindered Beaumarchais's efforts. The detailed exposition of the authors' grievances set forth by him in the *Compte rendu
de l'affaire des auteurs dramatiques et des comédiens français* did
not improve much the existing situation. However, thanks to his
continued struggle on behalf of the authors, the National Assembly
enacted a law in 1791 granting them the full ownership of their
works.

In 1779, Beaumarchais undertook to publish the complete works
of Voltaire. Although they were banned in France, Maurepas, a
minister of Louis XVI, unofficially endorsed the project after
Beaumarchais had succeeded in convincing the French not to allow
themselves to fall behind the Empress Catherine II of Russia, who
was prepared to publish an edition of Voltaire's works in St.
Petersburg.[29] In order to avoid a confrontation with the government,
Beaumarchais established a printing firm called *Société philosopht-
que, typographique et littéraire* at Kehl, a territory under the
jurisdiction of the Margrave of Baden. One of the obstacles that lay
initially in the way of the enterprise was a request by the Margrave
to omit from the edition all that was offensive to religion and morality in the writings of Voltaire. As a great admirer of Voltaire,
Beaumarchais considered such a request sacrilegious. He wrote to
the Margrave that Voltaire's works were expected by all Europe in
their totality. "M. de Voltaire," writes Beaumarchais, "was the first
man of our century who had opinions of his own. He expressed them
with all the philosophic freedom and exquisite taste of which he has
always been a model. What blasphemy is there to be found in all
that? He has expressed his feelings about all governments and all
sects, and, his great system being universal tolerance, one can omit
nothing from the works of this great man without weakening the
whole body of it."[30] The project was completed in 1790, not without
enormous losses being incurred by Beaumarchais, who sold only two
thousand copies of the fifteen thousand that were printed.

Beaumarchais also found time for pure business speculations. In
1785, he founded, with the help of the Périer brothers, both
engineers, the *Compagnie des Eaux de Paris,* which supplied Paris
with the water of the Seine by means of a steam pipe. As the shares
of the company increased, jealous financiers sought to undermine
Beaumarchais's enterprise. Claiming that water drawn from wells

was cheaper, they asked the Comte de Mirabeau to write a pamphlet to that effect. In need of money, Mirabeau accepted and thus drew Beaumarchais into a fresh polemic.

In 1792, Beaumarchais learned of the existence of sixty thousand guns for sale in Holland. Although he was reluctant to enter into new speculations, he declared his willingness to negotiate the deal, seeing in it a certain profit as well as an opportunity to serve the new revolutionary government which was in dire need of weapons. Inexplicably, Beaumarchais was accused in the Assembly of hiding the guns, and the infuriated people of Paris searched his house in vain. Beaumarchais soon realized that the corrupt ministers of the government were empowering him to acquire the guns on the one hand while trying to take away the deal from him on the other. He was arrested and miraculously escaped the terrible massacres of September, 1792, thanks to the efforts of a former mistress, who obtained his freedom. Beaumarchais tenaciously decided to proceed with his mission. He traveled to the Hague but was forced to leave upon learning on arrival that the minister Lebrun, who had issued a passport to him, had simultaneously ordered his arrest. Seeking refuge in London, he borrowed money from an English friend in order to purchase the guns. He was also prepared to return to France to plead his case before the Assembly in view of new accusations voiced against him. Seeing the danger that such a step would entail, Beaumarchais's friend had him arrested for debt. In prison, Beaumarchais wrote what he called "the six epochs of the nine most painful months of my life," where he recounts the whole episode of the guns affair. Six thousand copies of those mémoires were distributed in Paris. Having cleared his debt, he returned to France and, at the peril of his life, justified himself before the Assembly. Having been found innocent, he was appointed commissioner of the Republic and entrusted anew with the mission of obtaining the guns while receiving no money to purchase them. His task was further complicated by the fact that the guns were deposited in Holland, which had declared war on France and would not allow them to be shipped to an enemy. Beaumarchais sought to buy them through a third party, but he was not successful, for they had been acquired by the English. During a new stay in England he was declared persona non grata, and learned that the French considered him an émigré, a status that barred him from France. He sought refuge in Hamburg, where he lived in isolation until he returned to France in 1796.

V *Contested Plays*

In his preface to the *Barbier de Séville*, Beaumarchais ironically states that his reason for turning to comedy was due to the fact that the public was unable to appreciate his two dramas, *Eugénie* and *Les Deux Amis*. Indeed, the first could be played only after he rewrote its last two acts, and the second did not outlast its tenth performance.

Beaumarchais's talent expressed itself with far more success in his two comedies which cost him, nevertheless, many a battle. The *Barbier de Séville* stood ready as early as 1772. As a comic opera, it was refused by the Comédie-Italienne, a group of Italian actors playing in France. Thereupon, Beaumarchais was convinced by his friends to transform it into a comedy, which he read calmly in a salon on the evening following his altercation with the Duc de Chaulnes. The censorship had even approved it for production by the Comédie-Française in 1773, but the approval was reversed following Beaumarchais's imprisonment at the For-Lévêque. In 1774, authorization was granted again with the actors of the Comédie-Française showing much eagerness to play the work of the author who had just gained such a spectacular victory over Goezman. Authorization was withdrawn again when it was learned that Beaumarchais's comedy alluded to his recent trials. Beaumarchais vigorously protested, requesting the Parlement to examine the play and judge whether it was offensive in any way. After the dismissal of the Parlement Maupeou and the death of Louis XV, Beaumarchais was no longer compelled to suppress the allusions to his trials. When the play was finally presented on February 23, 1775, it proved too long, however, and Beaumarchais had to eliminate one full act. It soon acquired its well-known fame. The production was interrupted again after thirty-two performances, when the actors refused to present an accurate statement of accounts concerning the proceeds of the *Barbier* requested by Beaumarchais.

The battle of the *Mariage de Figaro* was no less eventful. In presenting Figaro rebelling against his master, Beaumarchais was, in a way, challenging royal authority. Upon completing the play in 1780, he requested that it be reviewed by censorship. The comedy aroused immediate interest and was even read at Court. Louis XVI is known to have said: "It is hateful, it will never be played. The Bastille would have to be destroyed before it could be performed. That man [Beaumarchais] mocks everything that is to be respected in government." Whenever Beaumarchais read the *Mariage* in the various salons, he knew how to emphasize its important points with a dramatic talent. A subtle conspiracy arose in favor of the play, while the author maintained that it was meant chiefly to entertain. In 1783, permission for its performance was granted but withdrawn suddenly on June 13 of the same year, just before curtain time. In September it was authorized only for the members of the Court. Finally, on April 27, 1784, the *Mariage de Figaro* had its opening night at the Comédie-Française, after it had been reviewed by six censors. One of them by the name of Suard, who had refused the play, continued to attack the author. Beaumarchais made it known that he would no longer reply, especially after he had to fight "lions and tigers" in order to win permission for his play to be presented. The king felt that Beaumarchais was including him in this phrase and sent him to prison. Such an arbitrary decision incensed those who had followed the four-year struggle that had just been won by the author of the *Mariage*. On the fifth day of his incarceration, Beaumarchais was freed with the apologies of the weak king.

In 1787, the opera *Tarare* was criticized at its dress rehearsal for denouncing despotism. *Le couronnement de Tarare,* an ending added to the opera in 1790 in order to adapt it to the political climate of the French Revolution, drew more criticism. Liberals regretted that Tarare, the new king, wished the negro slaves happiness instead of freeing them, while reactionaries felt that the question should not have been raised at all. As for *La Mère coupable,* a sequel to the comedies presented in 1792, it owed its short life only to the fame of the author.

Beaumarchais never accepted defeat in his battles. The author of the *Mémoires* had to convince public opinion that justice was on his side. The playwright had to prove that his art had an ethical intent. Even if such lofty claims were not always apparent or warranted, he exerted all the powers of his imagination to justify himself or his works. It is the literary value of his writings that will occupy our attention in the forthcoming chapters.

CHAPTER 2

Self-Defense As An Art

THE life of Beaumarchais appears as a vast trial. Surrounded by numerous enemies, he often finds himself isolated and must act as his own lawyer. Even when he chooses to defend victims of injustice other than himself, he identifies with them to the extent that their cause becomes his own. Rather than relying on the integrity of judges who can be swayed easily, he prefers to mobilize public opinion. This is why he published nearly all the mémoires he wrote in connection with his trials. In order to convince his audience of the justness of his case, he enters into lengthy explanations and details and subjects himself to an infallible reasoning. This is perhaps the tedious aspect of these mémoires. Yet, to Beaumarchais, all means are helpful. In his polemical writings, he resorts to eloquence, sentiment, sarcasm, wit, comedy, and drama, which often transform them into art.

I Against Goezman

Lintilhac considers the five mémoires concerning the Goezman affair as five acts of a classical tragicomedy.[1] This ingenious view emphasizes the unity of these writings and allows a systematic analysis of their structure. While the *Mémoire à consulter* can be read as a clear exposition of the facts, it does not lack witty and dramatic moments. Beaumarchais is outraged by the price of a first interview he seeks with Goezman. Five people are used as intermediaries to forward the money, and he writes: "Thus, from M. de Goezman to me there is a chain of seven people of which he pretends that I hold the first link as a corrupter and he the last as incorruptible" (253). Beaumarchais describes his futile attempts to see Goezman a second time despite the fact that he sent a diamond clock and an additional fifteen louis. Then, he presents the protagonists. There is Lejay, a friend of Madame Goezman, to whom he handed over the money according to her instructions, and who stated later, at the request of Goezman, that Beaumarchais had tried to corrupt a judge. There is Arnaud de Baculard, who supported Goezman's efforts by encouraging Lejay to maintain his false testimony. There is Marin, who, in order to please Goezman, influenced Bertrand Dairolles, another intermediary, to change his truthful testimony into a false one, and who advised an indignant Beaumarchais to drop the whole matter of the fifteen louis.

Lejay is depicted as so frightened by the situation he has brought upon himself that he hurries to admit the truth. Bertrand is shown torn between falsehood and truth. Marin promises to no longer exert pressure upon Bertrand. Madame Goezman herself is suspicious in the eyes of Parlement. Yet, Beaumarchais is not cleared. He does not deny that he gave her money. He insists, however, that he acted out of desperate necessity rather than attempting to corrupt a judge. Had he wanted to do so, he would have used a more direct method rather than one requiring the services of intermediaries. He concludes: "Therefore, it is on the hand that receives that justice should keep an eye and not on the hand that gives" (260).

In the *Supplément au mémoire à consulter,* Beaumarchais describes the tactics of his enemies. Madame Goezman claims that Lejay never presented her with any money intended for her husband, who is known to be incorruptible. Such an attitude can only excite the imagination of Beaumarchais, the playwright, who transforms into a comical sketch the confrontations that took place between him and Madame Goezman before the judge. In this sketch, Madame Goezman is the main character. She begins by disqualifying all witnesses that have some type of a relationship with Beaumarchais. When Madame Lejay testifies that Madame Goezman once admitted to her that she and her husband could not sustain themselves without bribes, "she blushes, becomes silent, daydreams for a long time, listens again to the testimony . . ., blushes again, becomes confused, asks for a glass of water . . ." and changes the subject completely. As for the fifteen louis, she declares: "it is no one's business, it concerns only M. Lejay and myself" (263). When she is asked to voice her complaints against Beaumarchais, she declares that he is an "atrocious" man and that she had never been approached on his behalf. When Beaumarchais in turn asks her to clarify her self-contradictory statements, she replies that they are due to her menstrual discomfort, and Beaumarchais writes: " ' Menstrual discomfort aside, madame,' I said to her, lowering my eyes on her behalf, 'this reason for your denial seems to me a little peculiar' " (267). Thus, by stressing Madame Goezman's foolishness and by ridiculing her, Beaumarchais has skillfully disposed of her.

With Goezman himself, Beaumarchais can no longer indulge in amusing sketches. A more serious attack is necessary, for, as John Hampton writes, "here the enemy is powerful, cunning and merciless."[2] Beaumarchais must separate the magistrate from the man, for, while he respects the former, he must expose the falsehoods of the latter. He shows that Goezman wrote for Lejay a first declaration stating that Madame Goezman had rejected the money and the clock and intimidated him into signing it. Subsequently, he had him sign a second one stating that no money was ever retained for the secretary or any other person, thus eliminating indirectly the whole question of the fifteen louis, the sole object of litigation. No credence can therefore be given to Goezman and his cowardly friends, while he, Beaumarchais, can boast of his honesty and amiability, as he expresses it in the following self-portrait: "You, my friends, who have known me, who have constantly followed me, have you ever seen in me someone else but a man always gay, who likes study and pleasure with an equal passion; prone to scoffing at others, but without bitterness, and accepting it equally from them; who supports his opinions with too much energy perhaps when he believes he is right; who holds in high esteem those he recognizes as superior to him; self-confident about his interests to the extent of neglecting them; energetic when stimulated, lax and sluggish after the storm; light-headed in the midst of happiness, but loyal and serene in adversity to the amazement of his most familiar friends" (281).

Beaumarchais's dramatic situation has now gained momentum because his enemies have been circulating pamphlets against him. He replies to them in the *Addition au supplément du mémoire à consulter*. Beaumarchais feels that Madame Goezman's pamphlet does not deserve much attention for it is packed with insults and material extraneous to the case. However, when she wishes to degrade him by writing that he is only a watchmaker's son, he says to her: "Forced to pass judgment on this point, I must admit with grief that nothing can absolve me of your just reproach that I am my father's son . . . But I must stop because I feel that he stands behind me seeing what I write and smiles while embracing me" (288). As for her claim concerning her husband's unquestionable integrity, Beaumarchais feels that it cannot be taken seriously for Goezman is known to have said about the trial: "one has judged the man rather than the case." He denounces Baculard who likes to circumvent the truth by devious ways. He demonstrates that Marin is not his friend as he pretends to be but rather Goezman's. Bertrand's oscillations between truth and falsehood seem to result from a curious conformation of his brain. Beaumarchais writes: "Here is a nice subject for the prize of the Academy of Surgery in 1774. One could win the medal by explaining how the brain of poor Bertrand could have suddenly split in two equal halves and produce in his head a memory so accurate on certain facts, so inaccurate on others . . ." (302). Beaumarchais also denounces Nicolai, a magistrate who counsels Goezman, for it is prohibited to do so when a judge is under investigation. He protests against his rival La Blache for accusing him falsely of seeking the protection of the daughters of Louis XV, while Beaumarchais had only asked them to certify that he was an honest man. A final blow is dealt at Goezman, when Beaumarchais unmasks him as a forger at the conclusion of this mémoire. He has discovered that his enemy fathered an illegitimate child of which he has declared himself the godfather under a false name. Thus, all respect should be withheld from this so-called representative of justice.

In the *Requête d' atténuation,* Beaumarchais summarizes his stand. This mémoire is chiefly devoted to proving that it is no crime for an innocent litigant to offer a judge money when this is the sole means of gaining access to him. Yet, at the same time, Beaumarchais maintains that it is a crime for a judge to accept it, and, to this effect, he quotes laws of the French judicial system going back to 1302. Lintilhac justly compares this *Requête* to a fourth act of a classical drama because it lacks dramatic progression and merely leads the reader into the last mémoire.

The introduction to the *Quatrième Mémoire à consulter* consists of an invocation addressed to the Supreme Being. Beaumarchais realizes that God has blessed him with good fortune in everything. He acknowledges, therefore, that some misfortune should befall him, and this can be nothing else but his trial. Far from rebelling, he accepts his fate with humility and even gratitude for having been given foes against whom he can justify himself easily. The ironical character of this invocation gives Beaumarchais the opportunity to pass his enemies in review once more before he disposes of them. Rather than facing the embarrassment of contradictory statements and uttering insults, Madame Goezman should have remained true to her feminine nature, which he found charming at the time of their confrontations, much to her delight. By supplying false information about himself on the birth certificate of his illegitimate child, Goezman has offended both Church and State which consider such a document essential to the future well-being of the child. Thus, it becomes easier to conceive how Goezman forged Lejay's declaration as well. Bertrand's credibility should be regarded as doubtful since he showed himself prone to falsehood in a previous dispute with Beaumarchais. He should be considered a mere instrument of Marin. Contrary to the latter's desire and advice, Beaumarchais is much interested in publicizing his present trial since it may help the Court to purge itself of some undesirable judges. As a president of the Court, Nicolai should never have humiliated Beaumarchais by angrily ordering his expulsion from the courthouse as he did on a certain occasion. Such behavior can only be explained by this magistrate's friendship with Goezman.

Beaumarchais also shows himself appearing before the Court, of which he gives the following theatrical description: "Upon viewing the courtroom which resembles a temple, the few lights which give to it a majestic and somber aspect, the stateliness of an assembly of sixty magistrates uniformly clad and all the eyes fixed upon me, I was seized with a most profound respect" (333). The Court requires Beaumarchais to answer questions by yes or no, and he complies with this request to the best of his ability. However, when he is asked whether he gave money to Madame Goezman, he must qualify his reply in the following way: "Yes, I have given money in order to obtain interviews with Monsieur Goezman; No, I have not given money in order to bribe him . . ." (334).

The hardest hit by Beaumarchais's invectives is Marin, a correspondent for various domestic and foreign newspapers and a pamphleteer. Originally a friend of Beaumarchais, he was now writing defamatory articles against him in order to please Maupeou and Goezman. Beaumarchais has already portrayed Marin in the gallery of his enemies presented in this mémoire. However, he wishes to give him a final thrust by drawing a forceful caricature of him. Marin has changed much since he was an innocent choir boy in his hometown. Now, he builds and destroys reputations at his whim, and Beaumarchais writes: "Eloquent writer, skillful censor, veracious newsmonger, hack journalist; when he crawls on the ground, he slithers along like a serpent; when he rises up, he flops down like a toad. In short, dragging himself along and climbing up by leaps and bounds, but always with his belly on the ground, he has done so well by his daily toils that nowadays we find the bandit going to Versailles. . . ."[3]

It is also Marin who was responsible for circulating an unsigned letter revealing that, during his stay in Spain, Beaumarchais had extorted at gunpoint from Clavijo a written promise of marriage for his sister Lisette. In the guise of a reply, Beaumarchais retells this whole episode at the close of his mémoire, turning himself into the hero of his own drama. He has traveled to Spain to avenge the honor of his sister not only at the behest of his father but also with the blessing of the princesses and Pâris-Duverney. Claiming to be on a literary mission, Beaumarchais gains access to Clavijo who feels very flattered by the visit. Beaumarchais tells him at length the story of a gentleman who has broken his engagement to a young lady. While she has taken the matter to heart, her brother has chosen to avenge her. Beaumarchais notices that Clavijo shows growing signs of uneasiness when he slowly recognizes himself as the protagonist of the story. Beaumarchais concludes it by saying that he himself is that brother, while Clavijo is the traitor. At that point, Beaumarchais draws of him the following portrait: "One can imagine the amazement of that man, stupefied by my harangue, opening his mouth in surprise and becoming unable to utter a word; one can imagine his radiant countenance brightened by my praise, gradually darkening, his eyes becoming dimmer, his features drawn out, his complexion dull" (348). Having been falsely accused by Clavijo of threatening him with a pistol, Beaumarchais seeks to justify himself. He concludes the episode by telling of his audience with the king of Spain who, upon hearing Beaumarchais's impassioned relation concerning the reasons for his stay in Spain, removes Clavijo from his high office.

Beaumarchais's contemporaries were prompt in appreciating the mémoires against Goezman. Of Beaumarchais, Voltaire wrote to d'Alembert: "What a man! he combines everything, jest, seriousness, reason, gaiety, forcefulness, feeling, all types of elo- quence, while not seeking any of them; he confuses his enemies and gives lessons to his judges."[4] To several other correspondents, he declared himself especially delighted by the fourth mémoire,[5] and to d'Argental he wrote: "I would advise Beaumarchais to stage his mémoires, in case his *Barbier* fails."[6] Upon hearing the rumor cir- culated by Marin, according to which Beaumarchais was not the author of his writings, Rousseau said: "I do not know whether or not he composes them, but I do know that one does not write such mémoires for someone else."[7] Forseeing Beaumarchais's career as an author of comedies, Bernardin de Saint-Pierre wrote to him: "Be convinced that I am paying to you all the tribute due to a man of letters who is expected to reach the heights of Molière's reputation. . . ."[8]

The court of Louis XV was so amused by those mémoires that Madame du Barry devised little sketches based on the confrontations between Madame Goezman and Beaumarchais. Concerning the effect the mémoires created in Europe, it will suffice to mention that Goethe based his *sturm und drang* play *Clavigo* of 1774 on the fourth mémoire, although he turned Clavigo, the protagonist, into a romantic hero. Elaborating later on that play in his *Either/Or*, Kierkegaard was able to analyze the subtle dialectic of "reflective love" such as it is felt by Marie Beaumarchais.

The *Mémoires* against Goezman have withstood the test of time, and, along with Beaumarchais's two comedies, they remain the best known of his works. In the realm of polemical literature, Lintilhac draws an interesting parallel between those writings and Pascal's *Provinciales*. He writes: "Pascal wants us to become serious about a cause of which he first exposes all the gaiety, while Beaumarchais wants to make us laugh about a cause the seriousness of which is never forgotten: the two methods are symmetrical while opposite."[9] It is somewhat pretentious to compare both works. Bearing upon the very nature of Christianity, the *Provinciales* are of interest to mankind. While having contributed to the downfall of a tyrannical Parlement, the *Mémoires* against Goezman merely relate the struggle of an individual against corrupt judges.

II *Against La Blache*

Beaumarchais had now to reply to La Blache who was still trying to win his case, which was being reviewed by the Parlement of Aix-en-Provence. La Blache characterized the case by the formula "Beaumarchais payé ou pendu" meaning either Beaumarchais was right and must be paid or he was wrong and must be hanged. Beaumarchais did not need more of an incentive to go on showing how much he was right. In his mémoires against La Blache, he proves that the statement of accounts, drawn up between him and Pâris-Duverney and contested by La Blache for its accuracy and authenticity, lay outside the jurisdiction of the first tribunal, for it was a document established in due legal form. Nevertheless, he does give a detailed exposition of his financial dealings to the extent that he rightly apologizes to his reader at one point, for presenting him a mémoire replete with figures.

Yet, beneath this network of proofs and demonstrations, one recognizes again the many facets of Beaumarchais's style as an author of mémoires. When Beaumarchais asks La Blache to pay him, the latter replies that he owes him nothing and denies that dealings have ever taken place between Beaumarchais and Pâris-Duverney. When Beaumarchais presents La Blache with the statement of accounts, he says that it is a rag. When Beaumarchais asks him to explain his contention, he answers that there were no dealings. When Beaumarchais asks him once again to clarify, he replies again that the statement is a rag, and Beaumarchais goes on recording this amusing conversation which revolves around the vicious circle in which his rival is caught. However, Beaumarchais knows how to become serious again. Amid the tedious task of defending himself, he still finds consolation in the thought of fighting injustice above all. He writes: "Once I have reached this abstraction, rising above the humiliation of my state, I see in myself but the defender of a victimized man; then, my thought fills my existence, and the noblest ability of man unfolds and exerts itself freely" (378).

Such interchange between earnestness and humor is frequent in those mémoires. At the beginning of his *Réponse ingénue*, a reply to La Blache's accusations, Beaumarchais relates that a peddler knocked on his door trying to sell him his enemy's pamphlets, telling him that no one wants to buy them and that he cannot go on carrying them much longer. Having pity on him, Beaumarchais buys one of them and dismisses him gently. Upon reading it, Beaumarchais notices that La Blache does not have the courage to accuse him directly. When La Blache's lawyers designate him as the plaintiff, they use the impersonal pronoun "ON" rather than his name. This entitles Beaumarchais to refer to his enemy as "Le Seigneur ON." Beaumarchais goes on telling how La Blache did everything he could to keep the dying Pâris-Duverney from seeing him. Both had to devise a clandestine system of correspondence in which Beaumarchais passed as a lover writing to his mistress, "the dear little one." He depicts the anguish of the old man becoming more and more dependent upon his designated heir whom he feared. Such a tragic end, Beaumarchais thinks, should serve as a lesson to those "pleasure-loving, freedom-seeking, and careless bachelors" who violate nature and society by refusing to marry, and he takes the opportunity to make an ardent plea in favor of fatherhood.

Beaumarchais feels that he can meet any of the challenges that may arise in his feud with La Blache. Unlike his rival who enlists lawyers, tries to bribe judges, and seeks to beguile the public, Beaumarchais will struggle alone. This attitude explains the mythical portrait he draws of himself at the conclusion of the *Réponse ingénue* where he writes: "As for myself, resembling the Tartar, the ancient Scyth a bit wild, always attacking in the field with a light weapon in his hand, I fight naked, alone, exposed . . ." (436). Indeed, the last mémoire is entitled *Le Tartare à la légion*, which suggests that Beaumarchais, comparing himself to a Tartar, is now facing the legion of La Blache and his aides. For the latter, Beaumarchais has only contempt and will be satisfied to address himself to their chief alone. Thus, after having proved once more that all of La Blache's accusations are unfounded, Beaumarchais unleashes against him the following apostrophe: "O perfidious and wicked adversary! How troublesome it is for me to unmask all your falsehoods as I learn them one by one! But you will not wear me out. I shall confuse you on every point . . ." (452). Beaumarchais is so sure of being in the right that he allows himself to display some conceit.

III   *Against Kornman*

The mémoires against Kornman consist mostly of the publication of his letters to Daudet de Jossan, the lover of his wife. By analyzing them and commenting upon them carefully, Beaumarchais shows that it is Kornman alone who is responsible for his wife's infidelity. The tone of these letters does not leave any doubt on that matter. In the midst of reading them, Beaumarchais feels compelled to warn Kornman on his intentions that appear too evident: "Beware Monsieur Kornman! One will say that you are advising two lovers to show decency in an affair approved by you! Beware! one shall say that you are subjecting your wife to the experience of a skillful seducer so that she may learn from him how to conduct a love affair without creating a scandal . . ." (459).

Upon reading further, Beaumarchais is appalled by the kindliness Kornman shows to Daudet de Jossan, and he exclaims: "O virtuous Kornman! scrupulous husband, kindhearted father! the man who was corrupting everything in your household was your *dear friend* . . ." (460). Then, Beaumarchais notices the sudden change of style in the correspondence as soon as Daudet's friend, the Prince de Montbarrey, leaves the ministry. Daudet is no longer addressed as "cher ami" but rather as "Monsieur," and Beaumarchais wonders: "Why are not our ministers irremovable? The friendships of our Guillaumes [Kornman] would certainly last eternally! . . ." (465).

In these mémoires, Beaumarchais's strict reasoning is again at work. To prove that a genuine attempt at a reconciliation with his wife was made on his part, Kornman claims that he wrote to her no less than two hundred letters over a period of fifty-four days, and he asks Beaumarchais to publish them along with the others. Yet, it is an easy matter to show that Kornman had written only five letters in a style that is far from being affectionate. Beaumarchais writes: "It was evident to us that one does not write two hundred letters in fifty-four days even to one's own mistress, let alone to a wife that is believed to be someone else's mistress . . ." (497).

Beaumarchais is able to clear himself of any accusation brought against him by Bergasse, the author of Kornman's pamphlets. This explains the amount of material extraneous to the case contained in those mémoires. At any rate, Beaumarchais seems to have been genuinely moved by the fate of Madame Kornman, and sentimentality is a distinctive characteristic of those writings. As an honest and sensible man who was made aware of Kornman's dealings, Beaumarchais feels compelled to help Madame Kornman. When he meets her for the first time upon visiting her in prison, he sees her wrapped in a shabby blanket, "pale, disturbed, pregnant, and beautiful." She recognizes him at once among the other visitors, falls to his feet, and cries. Beaumarchais himself is so moved, that he can barely comfort her. He concludes this tableau by writing: "I have witnessed this scene, I was part of it, I was part of it myself; I shall never forget it" (468). Madame Kornman's misfortune also affords Beaumarchais the opportunity to proclaim his long affection for women. At the end of the first mémoire, he writes: "I would be ungrateful, if I refused to help, in my old age, this beloved sex which made my youth happy!" (469).

IV *Against Lecointre*

The *Six Epoques* are six chapters of a mémoire preceded by a *pétition* addressed to the Convention Nationale. They constitute Beaumarchais's reply to the deputy Lecointre, who accused him of retaining sixty thousand guns acquired in Holland on behalf of the government. Sainte-Beuve is essentially right when he finds these writings boring,[10] for they represent a verbose and repetitive account of Beaumarchais's efforts to obtain the guns. Throughout the *Six Epoques,* he harps on the issue of the caution money he tried to secure from the French government in order to have the embargo on the guns lifted. He must prove that he did all he could to close the deal under the best possible circumstances and that the ultimate failure of the enterprise is due to the negligence and corruption of the ministers themselves.

In fact, Beaumarchais himself realizes that his mémoire is tiresome. At one point, he writes: "Let us stop! I feel that my reader is becoming weary" (562). Yet, he feels compelled to go on in order to rid himself of his frustration. Addressing himself once again to his readers, he says: "O citizens, swallow the tediousness of this discussion. It is not in order to amuse you that I am writing, but rather to convince you" (563). Occasionally, such frustration changes into indignation which is expressed in a lyrical tone. When he recalls the empty government offices where he had gone to present his request, he writes: "In a state that I cannot describe, I cried out involuntarily: O poor France! O poor France! And I returned home with a heart so heavy that I almost choked" (552). Upon realizing that his repeated efforts are of no avail, he dares to express his contempt even for the new political regime in these words: "Why are we to feel all the abuses of the old republics at the birth of ours? May I lose all my possessions, may I die rather than crawl under such insolent despotism!" (578).

In the "Quatrième époque," Beaumarchais enlivens his account when he relates his encounter with the individual who tried to persuade him to share the deal with him. Here, Beaumarchais is again creating an amusing scene with dramatic skill. When he is told that the embargo could be lifted if he were to agree to an increase in the price of the guns, he feigns to show interest in the proposal with the sole intention of sounding out its nature. Then, he tells his visitor that, on second thought, he does not see much advantage in the proposed partnership owing to the already too high costs of the enterprise. At this point, Beaumarchais is prompted to reconsider his attitude in view of an imminent warrant for his arrest. Beaumarchais now fully understands the nature of the offer which must originate from none other then Lebrun, the minister of foreign affairs, who is the only one able to supply the money as well as threaten him with arrest. Thus, the dénouement of this sketch is really the unmasking of Lebrun's hypocrisy.

André Hallays sees in the *Six Epoques* an interesting historical document which depicts dramatically the vileness and incoherence of government bureaucracy under the Revolution.[11] Beaumarchais relates, indeed, that an interview held between a minister and himself was constantly being interrupted by intruders (561). The authority of the ministers themselves is short-lived, and they "succeed each other as in a magic lantern" (567). If Lebrun entrusts Beaumarchais with the mission of concluding the sale of the guns, he forbids the French ambassador in Holland to accompany him to secure them, and Beaumarchais exclaims, "O disorder! O contradiction! I swear that everything works that way in this fatal department" (603).

In exposing his arguments, Beaumarchais also draws some interesting portraits. The issuing of a certificate clearing him of false accusations is suddenly held up by "a little man with black hair, a hooked nose, a frightful look who came in and whispered to the President. . . . Shall I tell you, O my readers! it was the great, the just, in a word the clement MARAT" (574). In the course of an interview with Lebrun, Beaumarchais stresses the latter's hypocrisy when he finds that his eyes "are a bit roving, his speech drawn out, and his voice faltering" (578). The following self-portrait depicts Beaumarchais's emotional strain at the time. Upon being freed from prison he goes directly to the office of Lebrun who is surprised to see him appear in his beautiful drawing room "looking like a prisoner, with a five-day stubble, disheveled, wearing dirty underlinen and only a frock coat . . ." (578). On an another occasion he shows himself appearing before a committee, and, asking for permission to come closer to the investigator who happens to be Danton, he uses his hand as an eartrumpet in order to hear better (586).

A sequel to the *Six Epoques* is a report to the Comité de Salut Public written by Beaumarchais on October 25, 1793, and recently published by Brian N. Morton.[12] In this report he recounts his dealings and wanderings with the intention of creating suspense. Such is for instance the account concerning the project of having the guns acquired from the Dutch by his English agent, who would sell them to his agent in Hamburg, who in turn would sell them to his agent in America, who would never receive them since the ship carrying the guns was to dock in a French port. Beaumarchais argues that he sought to ensure the success of the enterprise in this manner since the Dutch, being dependent on the Americans for their trade, would certainly not refuse them a sale. Beaumarchais writes to the members of the committee: "By taking all these precautions of high politics, I have remained, as you can see, the seller, the buyer, in short, the master of everything." It is interesting to note that, in this report, Beaumarchais speaks as if he had acquired the guns, whereas it is known that he was far from seeing that project realized.

V *Miscellaneous Memoirs*

In his *Observations sur le Mémoire justificatif de la Cour de Londres*, Beaumarchais undertakes the task of defending France's attitude and his own in the conflict that opposes England to her American colonies. He shows that despite the hostility England has always shown France, the latter remained neutral when the American insurrection broke out. However, France's neutrality could not extend as far as prohibiting French businessmen from dealing with the Americans. It is on that basis that Beaumarchais had undertaken to help the Americans despite the harassments that were inflicted on his ships by the English and even the French. The ultimate recognition of the United States by France was meant more as an acknowledgment of the reality of the situation than as a demonstration of hostility toward England. As for himself, he has continued to offer his help to the Americans at the cost of great financial losses. Yet, as he concludes, he hopes to have acquired the esteem of France, America, and even England. In this mémoire, Beaumarchais's reasoning is so strict that there is little room for the stylistic embellishments that enliven occasionally the argumentation of his other writings.

Beaumarchais reverts to his usual good humor in his *Compte rendu de l'affaire des auteurs dramatiques*. Fearing his campaign in favor of literary ownership, the actors inform him that, contrary to their policy toward other authors, they are willing to play his *Barbier de Séville* as many times as he wishes before claiming it as their own. Beaumarchais replies that he would like them to play it a thousand and one times. When the actors observe that he is rather "modest," he answers: "Modest, gentlemen, as you are honest! What is this mania of yours of seeking to inherit the property of those who are not yet dead" (619). The actors inform Beaumarchais that they are too busy with the Carnaval season to consider his proposals. Realizing that they are actually playing for time, he writes, "Allowing the actors and their lawyers to dance in peace, I waited patiently till the end of Lent; but either they were still dancing or making penance for having danced, I did not hear from any one" (625). Such gaiety, however, only helps to stress the seriousness of Beaumarchais's demands in favor of the authors for whom he seeks respectable retribution. He writes of them, "Too proud to accept charities, they are too destitute to suffer losses" (623). His program is designed to broaden the activities of the theater by introducing good plays on the stage, by seeking glory for the authors and success for the actors, by lowering the costs and increasing the profits. Appealing to the actors for their cooperation and good faith, he writes, "You are being applauded as men of talent; why don't you want to be praised as honest men, the only quality that remains for you to be acquired on this day?" (646).

When Beaumarchais is falsely accused of hiding wheat and guns in his cellars shortly before the outbreak of the Revolution, he writes the *Requête à Messieurs les représentants de la Commune de Paris*, where he proves that he is a faithful citizen. Indecently displaying his wealth, he announces that he is ready to pay large amounts of *écus* to anyone who can prove the veracity of the accusations voiced against him. His indignation forces him to adopt a grandiloquent tone throughout this mémoire. He recalls his previous trials and shows that he triumphed over his enemies in every one of them. He reminds his readers that he advised governments on the liberalization of the Parlement, was held in high esteem by princes, denounced despotism and defended Protestants and Jews against religious persecution.[13] He is particularly indignant when charged with greediness, while it is well known that his life has been "but a circle of generosity and charity" (527). Beaumarchais considers himself a victim of jealous men, and he asks the deputies of the Paris Commune to avenge him in the name of freedom.

Beaumarchais's irony sounds a bit exhausted when he replies to Mirabeau who wrote disparagingly concerning the activities of the Compagnie des Eaux de Paris. It allows him a mediocre pun on the *mirabelles* and *mirabilia* coming from Mirabeau. To show the advantages of the new enterprise that supplies Paris with water, Beaumarchais accumulates figures which he compares to those representing the costs of the old system. This makes rather dull reading, although the arguments remain convincing. Beaumarchais is happy to show that the so-called charlatanism of his company has resulted in an abundant flow of clean and inexpensive water that can be used in baths, laundries, industry, and animal drinking, greatly reducing the frequency of disease.

The unequal character of Beaumarchais's polemical writings has rightfully been pointed out. The stylistic luxuriance of the mémoires against Goezman is no longer the formula of the later mémoires, which are often burdened by repetition and excessive argumentation. Even the mémoires against Goezman are not exempt from such defects, and yet Beaumarchais can revert to sophisitication whenever the cause he defends dictates it. Such disparity is explained by the fact that Beaumarchais does not write his defenses according to a preconceived aesthetic scheme. They are rather the expression of his passionate feelings resulting from momentary circumstances that have affected him. Thus, while admiring the clear exposition and impeccable logic in these writings, one must also appreciate the voice of indignation, the power of irony, the comic scenes, the portraits, the caricatures—in short, Beaumarchais's ability to lighten his legal pleas with the ingredients of literary creation.

CHAPTER 3

Sensibility on the Stage

W HEN Beaumarchais devotes lyrical passages in his mémoires to the misfortunes of the childless Pâris-Duverney or those of Madame Kornman, he not only expresses his personal feelings but reacts as an *âme sensible,* a distinctive trait of the eighteenth-century man. He cultivates a literary tradition which, owing much to the works of Richardson, Diderot, and Rousseau, gave birth to a new theatrical genre, the drama. Beaumarchais begins his literary career as an author of two dramas, *Eugénie* and *Les Deux Amis.* He is so convinced of the authenticity and popularity of this genre that he writes a manifesto in defense of it. Although Beaumarchais's fame as a playwright lies much more in the two comedies that he wrote later, he reverts to *sensibilité* in his opera *Tarare* and in his last play *La Mère coupable.*

I *In Defense of the Drama*

Beaumarchais takes advantage of the presentation of *Eugénie* to write a long preface entitled "Essai sur le genre dramatique sérieux" in which he exposes his reasons for writing dramas. To Beaumarchais the classical theater seems highly unrealistic. It is governed by a set of rules that has more hindered than developed the creativeness of playwrights. The popularity of the works of Richardson and the dramas of Voltaire, Diderot, and Sedaine, has shown that the public is a more perceptive critic than those who judge a play according to its adherence to the rules of the classical theater. Beaumarchais undertakes, therefore, to compare the merits of the drama with those of the heretofore existing forms of theater, tragedy and comedy.

Tragedy inspires terror by its decor which represents death, blood, and ruins and by the catastrophic fate of its characters, who are mostly princes at the constant mercy of cruel gods. Its themes and situations are so far removed in time, its heroes of such a superior condition, and their sacrifices so gratuitous that it arouses at best a sterile admiration. Eighteenth-century man is not affected much more by comedy, because he remains more amused by the roguishness of its characters than uplifted by the lesson it supposedly teaches. On the contrary, drama or the *genre sérieux* presents a touching situation with which one can always identify. Its heroes are always honest and common people whose misfortunes not only arouse our compassion but force us to look into our own hearts. As an intermediary genre between tragedy and comedy, drama can be as sublime as the former since it also portrays man's struggle with life and does so more effectively than the latter, which presents only the perplexities in which he is caught up. Since tragedies and comedies are unnatural creations, they can be written in verse which contributes to their embellishment. Drama must find its eloquence in the reality of its situations. Its language is that of true passions and, therefore, does not need the ornaments of a flowery style.

Beaumarchais goes on to present *Eugénie.* He is convinced that its success lies in its subject, which is true to life. All characters are conceived so as to reinforce the conflict of Eugénie, the main protagonist. In order to emphasize the intensity of such conflict, Beaumarchais creates his characters so that their situations are in constant opposition with their desires. He also informs his audience on their nature and intentions leaving no room for unnecessary dramatic surprises. He states that he wishes to stir the emotions of the spectator out of the natural development of the dramatic situation, and if he succeeds in so doing, he will consider himself rewarded for his toils.

In presenting his theory of the drama, Beaumarchais is only reflecting the growing popularity this genre had acquired in the second half of the eighteenth century. He is not an innovator, however, since he mostly takes Diderot's ideas on the subject as they appear in *De la poésie dramatique* and *Entretiens sur le Fils Naturel.* Moreover, he does not see the majestic beauty of tragedy unlike Diderot, who believed in the rules of the classical theater and conceived the genre sérieux only as an intermediary step of a dramatic hierarchy consisting of the marvelous and the tragedy on the one hand, and of the comedy and the burlesque on the other.

It is a strange paradox to see Beaumarchais dismiss comedy so swiftly in view of the fact that his achievements in that genre were to become the most outstanding in the eighteenth century. He also exaggerates the importance of drama, which represents a rather simplistic form of art. Yet, Beaumarchais skillfully exploits the principle of the opposition between the situation of characters and their desires, which he will apply in his comedies as well. He exposes his theory with conciseness and precision, gives a detailed insight into the mechanism of his play *Eugénie*, and speaks of the new genre with a rare enthusiasm.

II Eugénie

As shown by Brian N. Morton, who discovered an edition of *Eugénie* bearing the date of 1762 on its title page, Beaumarchais is to be believed when he writes at the beginning of his "Essai" that *Eugénie* was completed about eight years before it was presented. This finding verifies Loménie's assertion that Beaumarchais is the first to have called his play a drama. It also indicates that it was conceived well before the Clavijo affair.[1] Thus, Beaumarchais was not prompted to write his play by the family incident but rather developed the theme of the seduced girl, which was very fashionable in the eighteenth century.

Baron Hartley, his daughter Eugénie, and Madame Murer, sister of the Baron, have arrived in London at the house of Count Clarendon. The Baron, unaware of his daughter's secret marriage to Clarendon, does not understand her sadness, as he intends to marry her to his elderly friend Cowerley. Madame Murer, who has brought up Eugénie since the death of her mother, opposes such a project and would rather see her niece's secret marriage become official. Eugénie admist to her aunt that she is uneasy about having concealed the marriage from her father. She also fears that Clarendon no longer loves her, for he is not even present to greet her. Madame Murer feels that Clarendon will love Eugénie more when he learns that she is pregnant.

Drink, the servant of Clarendon, announces the arrival of his master to Eugénie and Madame Murer. Yet, he feels guilty of not informing them that the Count is about to marry a rich woman according to the orders of an influential uncle. Drink reminds his master of the fact that his marriage to Eugénie was a sham, since it was performed by Williams, the Count's steward, disguised as a minister. While he is aware of his duplicity, Clarendon is determined to marry the rich woman. When he sees Eugénie again, he assures her of his love and persuades her to postpone revealing their secret to the Baron.

On orders from the Count, Drink has intercepted a letter written by Williams to Madame Murer, in which the steward tells of his remorse at having performed the false marriage. Drink must also see to it that Captain Cowerley, a brother of the Baron's friend, is not admitted to the house since he knows of Clarendon's forthcoming marriage. Yet, the captain succeeds in being admitted. He announces that Sir Charles, Eugénie's brother, is to fight a duel and is in need of protection. Considering Clarendon as her nephew's future brother-in-law, Madame Murer asserts that he would readily protect him. Hearing the name of Clarendon mentioned, the captain announces that he is about to be married. When Madame Murer declares that the Count has a previous engagement, the captain replies that he is well known for his frivolous attitude toward women. The news causes Eugénie to faint.

Having been made aware of the situation, the Baron reprimands his sister for having improperly raised Eugénie. Madame Murer remains convinced that Clarendon will respect his engagement toward Eugénie all the more since she is carrying his child. Baron Hartley is now willing that Eugénie marry Clarendon but wishes to clear up the matter of his forthcoming marriage. He questions Drink who tells the whole truth and shows Williams's letter. The Baron curses Eugénie, while Madame Murer urges her to write to Clarendon. Because Eugénie refuses to submit to such an indignity, Madame Murer writes the letter herself.

As Clarendon is expected, Madame Murer is determined to have him seized by armed men and forced to marry Eugénie, and she even has a minister ready to perform the ceremony. Clarendon arrives with Sir Charles whose life he has just saved. Unaware of Sir Charles's identity, he explains to him that he must justify his attitude toward a girl he has seduced, adding that he fears the vengeance of her brother. When confronted with Williams's letter in the absence of Sir Charles, Clarendon explains that he had to resort to a false marriage for fear of losing Eugénie when ordered by his uncle to marry someone else. When Sir Charles enters, he realizes that it is his sister who has been betrayed. Nevertheless, he protects Clarendon from the hands of the armed servants, and, feeling that he has repaid him the debt of his life, he challenges him to a duel in order to save the honor of his sister.

Eugénie, who still loves Clarendon, implores her brother not to kill him. Sir Charles is determined to avenge her. Suddenly, he returns announcing that the duel has not taken place since his sword broke. Clarendon arrives shortly after and convinces everyone of the sincerity of his repentance, which enables him to marry Eugénie.

At the end of each act, Beaumarchais introduced *jeux d'entracte* ("intermission scenes"). At the end of the first two acts, servants are putting in order the room where the action has taken place. At the end of the third act, preparations are made for the seizure of Clarendon according to Madame Murer's plan, and, at the end of the fourth act, Eugénie's family and servants comfort her after a breakdown. By keeping the attention of the audience on the play between the acts, Beaumarchais meant to stress its realism. Fearing the boldness of such innovation, the actors of the Comédie-Française refused to play those scenes, much to Beaumarchais's regret. Indeed, these jeux d'entracte remain within the fictional framework of the play and do not fulfill Beaumarchais's intention.

Eugénie suffers from several other weaknesses. Although Eugénie's outcries were exaggerated in a first version of the play, they remain excessive in the last one. As shown by Jacques Schérer, Clarendon is not really a scoundrel since it is rather for the sake of ambition than for lack of love that he thinks of abandoning Eugénie. Thus, the obstacle of this drama is not as insurmountable as we find it in classical tragedy.[2] The false marriage ceremony or the breaking of Sir Charles's sword are unlikely events. Finally, Beaumarchais is able to conclude his play only by attaching to its main plot a secondary one arising from the unexpected relationship between Clarendon and Sir Charles.

Yet, Beaumarchais shows some skillful qualities as a playwright. Although the exposition of *Eugénie* is not completed until the beginning of the second act, where Drink reveals the content of Williams's letter, such delay helps to increase the suspense which remains sustained at least until the end of the third act. During the first three acts, Eugénie remains a touching character, especially when she reveals her secret to her father. The situation that exists between

Clarendon and Sir Charles, and which may have been inspired by
Scarron's *Les Ennemis généreux*, is characterized by dramatic intensity.[3] While the dialogues are affected at times, they are lively and fit
the nature of the drama. *Eugénie* had a successful run on the stage,
an achievement which cannot be ascribed to Diderot's *Le Père de
Famille* and *Le Fils Naturel*, which are dramas that could hardly be
played and remain mere illustrations of his theories.

III Les Deux Amis ou le Négociant de Lyon

Dealing with an incident in the life of two businessmen, this play
is once again inspired by the ideas of Diderot who thought that con-
flicts arising from social conditions constitute choice material for
dramas.

The son of Mélac, and Pauline, the niece of Aurelly, who have
been raised together since childhood, are in love. Dabins, who is
Aurelly's cashier, informs Mélac, Aurelly's best friend, that his
master is unable to meet an unexpected debt of six hundred thousand francs because a debtor who was to send those funds died
leaving an estate not yet opened. Dabins cannot break the news to
Aurelly who would certainly take it to heart, for he firmly believes
that there is no greater disgrace for a businessman than that of being
unable to pay his debts. In fact, Aurelly forcefully conveys these
ideas to Mélac in the course of a conversation.

Aurelly's situation puts Mélac in a dilemma. As a Farmers' tax
collector for his district, he is in possession of the funds that could
save his friend's reputation. However, they are to be handed over to
Saint-Alban, the Fermier-général, who has arrived to collect them.
Mélac decides to help Aurelly and asks Dabins to keep the whole
matter a secret. When Saint-Alban requests the money, Mélac asks
him for a three-week delay to pay it. As a result, both Saint-Alban
and Aurelly become suspicious of Mélac's conduct.

Young Mélac explains to his father that Saint-Alban's hostility is
due to the fact that they are both rivals in their love for Pauline.
Mélac believes that Aurelly should be made aware of Saint-Alban's
feelings about Pauline since Aurelly could benefit much from their
marriage. Aurelly urges Mélac to explain the whereabouts of the
money. As Mélac is unable to do so, Aurelly quickly brands him as
an impostor. Mélac maintains that he is innocent, explaining that
honor alone forbids him to talk. Pauline is convinced of Mélac's

honesty and urges her uncle to pay his debt. Aurelly replies that he would do it if he did not have to retain some money for the dowry of a daughter born of a secret marriage. When Pauline learns that she herself is that daughter, she urges Aurelly again to use the entire funds at his disposal to save Mélac.

Saint-Alban, who had previously announced the approval of young Mélac as the successor of his father upon the latter's retirement, fears that he has sealed thereby the marriage between young Mélac and Pauline. He is jealous of him, demands payment of Mélac, and intends to report on his conduct. Aurelly offers to pay for Mélac and asks Saint-Alban to remain silent about the whole matter. He agrees, but chooses that moment to ask Aurelly for Pauline's hand. Pauline informs young Mélac that his father's debt will be paid by her uncle with money set aside for the dowry of his daughter born of a secret marriage. She also announces to him that Aurelly would like him to marry that daughter. Young Mélac becomes angry when he learns that a girl without a name is intended for him. Pauline then reveals her identity, afraid that young Mélac does not love her. While he assures her of his love, Pauline asks him to allow her to speak with Saint-Alban. Young Mélac fears that she will abandon him.

Pauline reproaches Saint-Alban for having agreed to keep silent about Mélac on the condition that she marry him. He replies that his agreement was unconditional, adding that he believes that she is not loved by young Mélac. Having overheard the conversation, young Mélac tells Saint-Alban that he renounces his love for Pauline only because of the misfortune that befell his father. As a tribute to the magnanimity of both young Mélac and Pauline, Saint-Alban withdraws as her suitor. Realizing that Aurelly is about to pay Mélac's debt with the money left in the hands of his Parisian debtor, Saint-Alban informs him that the latter has died and that the funds are unavailable at the moment. At this point, Dabins admits that he has never received the money and that Mélac has supplied funds to pay Aurelly's debt. Overwhelmed by the news, Aurelly announces that he will not take advantage of such a plan. However, Saint-Alban insists that Mélac's plan be maintained as he proposes to be Aurelly's creditor until his financial situation is cleared. The friendship of Aurelly and Mélac is sealed by the marriage of their children, and Saint-Alban leaves edified by the high moral standards of those virtuous families.

It is evident that in writing *Les Deux Amis* Beaumarchais could not follow Diderot's recommendations to the letter and build his play solely on the theme of the businessman. In order to give more substance to it, he had to introduce the romance between the children of the two friends. Here, as in *Eugénie,* verisimilitude is greatly sacrificed, for the play rests on such unrealistic data as the unavailability of Aurelly's funds or Mélac's obstinate silence. Furthermore, there is no real drama since the marriage between young Mélac and Pauline is only delayed by Mélac's situation, which is unknown to Saint-Alban. However, as shown by Jacques Schérer, as soon as Saint-Alban becomes aware of it, he does what is expected of him, namely renouncing his suit of Pauline and offering to be Aurelly's creditor.[4]

Yet, *Les Deux Amis* represents an improvement in relation to *Eugénie.* Anthony Pugh has shown that this drama approaches the ideal of the *pièce bien faite.*[5] The traditional recognition scene occurring in the drama does not represent a denouement, since we already learn at the end of the third act that Pauline is Aurelly's daughter. Suspense lies elsewhere. Beaumarchais has created it by building a sound exposition in the first act and by unfolding gradually before our eyes the elements of the delayed situation which forms the basis of his drama. He touchingly depicts the gentle love of the young people and has succeeded in his portrayal of Pauline, who knows how to recognize true love. Despite some obscurity, the dialogues are very vivacious. It is true that the Parisian public did not appreciate the play which seemed too faithful a mirror of the business milieu. It was better received in the business towns, and Beaumarchais vowed eternal affection to *Les Deux Amis,* which he considered the best composed of all his plays.

IV   Tarare

Beaumarchais's ideas concerning opera are exposed in his preface to *Tarare.* He devised for it a formula that includes aesthetic, dramatic, and ethical considerations. Since opera must resort to several branches of the arts, he wishes to establish among them a hierarchy which would best express his own conception of opera. Priority should be given to the dramatic situation responsible for arousing interest, because the drama would be enhanced by the beauty of the poem by means of which it is expressed, and the poem would in turn be made more harmonious and charming by music and dance. Since opera is neither tragedy nor comedy, its subject should be of a genre that is both historical and supernatural. Finally, opera should have an ethical intent and proclaim the supremacy of virtue.

Such are the guidelines which presided over the composition of *Tarare*. The title of Beaumarchais's opera is the name of a character in *Fleur d'Epine*, a story by Hamilton, and was chosen simply because of its oddity. The plot is taken from *Sadak et Kalasrade*, a Persian tale in which a jealous tyrant takes away the wife of an obedient servant who is protected by a eunuch and who is proclaimed king against his will as a result of a rebellion. Thinking that the audiences of his days devoted too much interest to the music of opera, Beaumarchais chose to give preeminence to the dramatic situation and poetic language of *Tarare;* the role of its music was to be purely ornamental. This is probably the reason why the musician Gluck, seeing such a minor role for music, refused to collaborate with Beaumarchais on *Tarare* and suggested for the task his disciple Salieri, who proved more submissive.

The supernatural element of *Tarare* consists of an allegorical prologue. As for the historical element, Beaumarchais chose to set the action in an oriental environment at a time when despotism, violent passion, and ignorance could be sharply contrasted with supreme virtue. Beaumarchais stresses the fact that whatever pleasure the spectator was to derive from *Tarare*, he was not to forget that the main theme of the work was "the dignity of man."

In the prologue, the Genius of Fire questions Nature about her activities. She replies that she creates human beings out of shadows without being really concerned about their destiny. Thus, she has arbitrarily decided that one shadow would be a king and the other a soldier. While these shadows show no particular enthusiasm about their new condition, the Genius of Fire decides that one shadow should become the Emperor Atar, the despot of Asia, and the other should be Tarare, an unknown soldier. The other characters of this opera are created in the same arbitrary way. At the end of the prologue, the Genius of Fire and Nature express their eagerness to learn how these newly created beings of such dissimilar condition will deal with their life, and then they disappear.

In his palace at Ormus, Atar is extremely unhappy to see that Tarare, one of his soldiers, is so virtuous. He is also envious of the bliss Tarare has found in his marriage to Astasie. Therefore, Atar orders one of his generals, Altamort, who is the son of the High Priest Arthénée to seize Astasie. Arthénée encourages Atar to pursue a war that would consolidate his despotic power as well as the established religion, while maintaining the slaves in their chains. When the child Elamir is asked by Arthénée to prophesy about the future avenger of the Empire, he names Tarare. Atar is infuriated to witness the popularity of Tarare acclaimed by the assembled people.

Calpigi, the Emperor's chief eunuch, informs Tarare that Atar is prepared to marry Astasie. Both plan to kidnap her from the Emperor's harem, and, to this end, Calpigi prepares a silken ladder which will enable Tarare to penetrate into the harem. While Calpigi entertains the Emperor, who is about to crown the reluctant Astasie empress, Tarare descends the silken ladder. Taking advantage of the privacy Atar is seeking with Astasie, Calpigi hides Tarare in the garb of a mute slave. Atar returns angered by Astasie's disdain. To punish her, he orders Calpigi to throw her into the arms of that despicable mute slave, much to Calpigi's contentment.

When Astasie is ordered by Atar to marry the slave, she asks her servant Spinette to take her place. Spinette agrees, soon unmasks Tarare, and even falls in love with him. Thereupon, soldiers arrive with orders to arrest the mute slave. Although Tarare reveals his identity to them, they insist on carrying out their orders. Tarare and Astasie must die. Their love expressed in the face of death angers Atar. At this moment, the rebellious army led by Calpigi wants to proclaim Tarare king. He refuses, swearing to remain faithful to the Emperor. Embittered by the events, Atar kills himself. Tarare becomes king against his will and declares that he will remain a slave to his country. The opera ends with the reappearance of the Genius of Fire and Nature, who proclaim that the greatness of man lies not in his social condition but in his character.

The ending of *Tarare* seems to have been a matter of constant adaptation according to the various political regimes in power. In the original denouement, Tarare vows to be an enlightened king. In *Le Couronnement de Tarare*, added in 1790 upon the occasion of the Fête de la Fédération, Tarare is a constitutional monarch who not only receives his power from the people but institutes legal divorce, marriage for priests, and eases the bonds of negro slaves. While Beaumarchais was an émigré at Hamburg, the ending became republican in spirit, since Tarare refuses the crown and proclaims the sovereignty of law and freedom of all citizens. In 1819, the opera ends with a reconciliation between Atar who remains the king and Tarare who becomes the chief of staff. Loménie writes: "After having been purely and simply monarchistic, then constitutionally monarchistic, then republican, *Tarare* was becoming even more monarchistic than at its beginnings."[6]

Despite its naive theme, *Tarare* had a rather successful career. According to Loménie, it aroused more curiosity than admiration. Yet, Beaumarchais had realized in this opera his idea of a *drame chanté* which pleased audiences of the time. Atar's ferociousness, which conceals inner torment and anguish, as opposed to Tarare's gentleness and confidence, represents an interesting contrast, which moves the spectator as well as holds his interest. The action is enhanced by the spectacular arrangement of scenery, costumes, music, and dance. Although the poetic language of *Tarare* is very dull, one ascribes to Beaumarchais the originality of having devised for opera a formula in which poetry decently supersedes the music.

In choosing the meaningless title *Tarare*, Beaumarchais intended to draw the attention of the public to the Manichaean nature of the drama. Indeed, the name Tarare infuriates Atar whenever he hears it, and it serves as a rallying cry to the rebels. Writing the history of that name, Jacques Schérer sees in it an illustration of Beaumarchais's ability to derive dramatic effects from certain names he gave to his characters.[7] Because of its theme, *Tarare* can also be considered an example of eighteenth-century *littérature engagée*, for it denounces tyranny and bigotry and extols, above all, human virtue.

V   La Mère coupable

Notwithstanding the fact that this play is a drama, Beaumarchais considered it a natural continuation of the *Barbier de Séville* and the *Mariage de Figaro*, since the characters of these two comedies reappear in it. In his preface to the play, he writes that he even welcomed the initiative of the actors of the Theâtre-Français, who wanted to stage the whole saga of the Almaviva family in three consecutive performances. By introducing the character of Bégearss (inspired by Kornman's lawyer Bergasse), a scoundrel because of whom the play is also entitled *L'Autre Tartufe*, Beaumarchais claims to have combined the intrigue of comedy with the emotional nature of drama. However, with *La Mère coupable*, Beaumarchais is really reverting to the drama genre he practiced in his first two plays. He states in the preface that his design is chiefly to move his audiences to tears by presenting them with a play that illustrates the basic goodness of man.

Count Almaviva lives alienated from his wife, the "guilty mother" of Léon, the offspring born twenty years ago of her liaison with Chérubin. Almaviva puts all his trust in Bégearss whom he has taken into his house. Bégearss, who knows the secrets of both the count and the countess, undertakes to divide the family. He would like to see the count divorce his wife, estrange Léon, and dismiss his old servant Figaro. He also seeks to marry Florestine, the natural daughter of Almaviva, who passes as an adopted child. Bégearss has succeeded in obtaining from Suzanne, the countess' chambermaid, the jewel box of the countess, which contains a bracelet bearing Almaviva's portrait once offered by him to his wife. Bégearss claims that the count would like to have a copy of it made for Florestine. Having examined the contents of the jewel box, Almaviva substitutes for the original bracelet, which he intends to give to Florestine, an identical one bearing the portrait of Chérubin. He explains to Bégearss that if the countess, confronted anew with her sin, will remain silent about the exchange, his suspicion about Chérubin will be confirmed. Bégearss, who had the jewel box made for the countess, knows that it has a double bottom and contains, in addition to the jewels, the countess' secret correspondence with Chérubin. He feigns to break it in front of the count thus exposing the correspondence. Almaviva retains one of the letters in which the countess informs Chérubin, who is fighting in the war, that she bore him a son but that, regretting her sin, she has decided no longer to see him. The letter bears Chérubin's reply written with his blood, in which he informs the countess that he is about to let himself be killed in the war.

When Bégearss realizes that Léon and Florestine are in love, he reveals to each one of them that they are brother and sister. He has also arranged for the property owned by the count in Spain to be exchanged for property in France where the count now lives. As

Almaviva's prospective son-in-law, Bégearss hopes to benefit from that property. He also intends to appropriate Florestine's dowry consisting of three million golden louis that Figaro has deposited in the hands of a notary hoping that Bégearss' hypocrisy will be discovered.

The countess does not understand the disarray that has suddenly invaded her family, namely, the count's isolation and the despair of Léon and Florestine. She consults Bégearss who explains to her that the count dreads what he believes to be an incestuous marriage between Léon and Florestine, who is really his daughter. On hearing the truth about Florestine the countess is somewhat relieved at the thought that her husband is also "guilty." She is grateful to Bégearss for this revelation and offers him her support concerning his project of marrying Florestine. Bégearss also persuades the countess to burn the correspondence she kept with Chérubin so that no evidence of her guilt will remain and the family may live in perfect harmony. He then informs Almaviva of this last achievement, which is really designed to expose the countess, since he knows that the letter proving her infidelity remains in the count's hands. As a reward, Bégearss obtains from the count the receipt enabling him to withdraw the three million louis held by the notary.

When Léon expresses to Bégearss his bitterness over the count's decision to estrange him, Bégearss advises him to ask his mother to intervene with the count on his behalf. The countess, who has lived in remorse over her sin for twenty years, is apprehensive about begging the count's solicitude for Léon. Yet, she arms herself with courage and decides to fulfill her son's desire. It is this moment that Almaviva has chosen to confront his wife with the letter proving her guilt. In the presence of the count, she touchingly confesses her sin and asks God for forgiveness. When Almaviva reminds her that she dares to wear her former lover's portrait on her bracelet, she believes she is having visions of Chérubin when she notices that his portrait has replaced that of her husband. The strain of the confrontation causes her to faint. Witnessing the sincerity of his wife's repentance, Almaviva forgives her.

The countess expresses her wish to finish her life in a convent and bids Almaviva happiness on the forthcoming marriage of his daughter to Bégearss. Seeing that Bégearss has revealed to the countess Florestine's identity, the count unmasks him as a hypocrite. Happiness for the family is complete once Figaro has cunningly succeeded in retrieving the three million louis from Bégearss and all acknowledge, against the latter's assertion, that Léon and Florestine are unrelated.

La Mère coupable is a complex play consisting of several plots. Bégearss' intrigues are successfully intertwined with the idyll between Léon and Florestine and the financial imbroglio resolved by Figaro. Of the dramatic structure of this play, Beaumarchais writes that it is one of the most solid ever conceived by him.[8] Gudin de la Brenellerie, Beaumarchais's biographer and friend, considers the play dramatically convincing and touching.[9] When it was presented in 1797 after Beaumarchais's return from exile, the audience asked for the author to appear on the stage to receive an ovation. As for Napoleon, he had no other name for Beaumarchais than that of "the author of *La Mère coupable*."

As can be seen from the concluding sentences of the preface, Beaumarchais was not unaware of the weaknesses of his play. The solidity of its structure does not conceal the melodramatic devices such as the double bottom of the jewel box, the intercepted letters, and, above all, Almaviva's sudden suspicion about his wife's infidelity after twenty years. One also wonders why the crafty Bégearss allows himself to be so childishly ensnared at the end of the play. The characters do not fulfill an essential dramatic function since they are overshadowed by Bégearss' shrewdness. Figaro, the touchstone of Beaumarchais's comedies, has not only grown old but is reduced to the role of spying upon Bégearss with the help of his wife Suzanne. The moving repentance of the countess, who is generally viewed as redeeming the play, remains the best of the many sentimental scenes of this *larmoyant* drama. As René Pomeau thinks, Bégearss would have been a more successful creation had he been ridiculed rather than transformed into a frightening figure.[10] Such was not Beaumarchais's intention, however, for he meant, rather, to have his audience go home with the satisfaction of seeing hypocrisy chastised.[11]

A great part of Beaumarchais's dramatic production belongs to the drama genre. Not only did he revert to it with his last play, but he intended to write a sequel to it to be entitled *La Vengeance de Bégearss ou le Mariage de Léon*. As an author of dramas, Beaumarchais remains quite faithful to the prevailing literary genre of his time and achieves in it a significant success. The weaknesses of these plays are much more inherent in the eighteenth-century *sensiblerie* than in Beaumarchais's capacity as a playwright. Besides, drama and comedy are by no means incompatible in his theater. It has been shown that, while writing his dramas and his opera *Tarare*, he was tempted to include in them strongly comic scenes that he eliminated only upon the insistence of his friends. On the other hand, one finds in the comedies sentimental scenes which cause the comic action to be temporarily suspended. Such a blending gives to Beaumarchais's theater its unity.

CHAPTER 4

Comedy in the Making

B EAUMARCHAIS'S career as an author of comedies originates
with the *Parades*, the bold little sketches he wrote for the social
circle of his friend Charles Lenormand d'Etioles. As Beaumarchais
deemed them unworthy of publication, they remained unknown until 1863. The *Parades* already contain characters, situations, and
dramatic devices that were to be fully developed in the comedies.
When the *Barbier de Séville* was hailed as an unchallenged success,
after the fiasco of its first performance, Beaumarchais wrote a
humorous preface for it in which he reviewed his past career as a
playwright, mocked the ill-intentioned critics of his play, and exposed his art. The theme of the *Barbier* can be traced as far as antiquity and recurs constantly as a subject of comedy throughout the
centuries. Yet, in his first comedy, Beaumarchais reveals himself as a
masterful craftsman in his construction of the intrigue, in the
joyfulness of his comic style, and in the creation of unforgettable
characters.

I The Parades

The *parade* is a sketch usually played by the actors of theaters
located on fairgrounds. It is performed outside the theater in order
to entice the public to attend the main performance. This genre
became increasingly popular at the end of the reign of Louis XIV,
when the people harassed by the miseries of that period, found some
distraction in such sketches. Following the model of the *commedia
dell' arte*, the parades were largely improvised. With the advent of
the eighteenth century, they were no longer meant to attract common folk only. Respectable authors tried their hand at them and
they were played in the salons. Dignitaries and noblemen seeking
the enjoyment of the lower classes attended the staging of parades in
disguise so as to conceal their identity and even to act in them.

Under their new aspect, these sketches were less improvised and featured the characters traditionally known in Italian or French comedy: Cassandre, Isabelle, Léandre, and Gilles. Their themes are often subtly obscene and their comic effect is further enhanced by the distorted language of the characters, who appear as boors and try to outwit each other.

It is difficult to determine precisely when Beaumarchais wrote his parades. The most plausible view on this point is that of Jacques Schérer, who thinks that they were composed between 1757 and 1763.[1] In 1756, Pâris-Duverney introduced Beaumarchais to Lenormand d'Etioles, whose wife, the Marquise de Pompadour, had been the mistress of Louis XV since 1745. To console himself for his conjugal misfortune, Lenormand entertained his pleasure-loving friends at his castle of Etioles. Beaumarchais seems to have enlivened the atmosphere of Etioles with the parades he wrote exclusively for the parties given at the castle. However, as of 1764, the two friends went their separate ways, as Beaumarchais became more and more engrossed in his financial dealings and Lenormand was allowed to remarry upon the death of Madame de Pompadour.

Colin et Colette is a short parade portraying a couple of young peasants having a lovers' quarrel. Colin has gathered a bouquet of flowers and tells Colette that they are not for her. Naturally, she suspects him of being unfaithful. Colin soon explains that the flowers are intended for the lord of the castle, who might have taken them away from Colette had he seen them in her hands. Colette realizes that Colin wants to spare her such an offense and regards his action as a proof of love.

Les Députés de la Halle et du Gros-Caillou is a parade of the *poissard* genre in which the protagonists are fishwives well known for their vulgarity. The fishermen Jérôme and Cadet wish to enter a castle in order to present the lord with their merchandise. Mère Fanchette and Mère Chaplu have arrived for the same purpose. While Mère Chaplu is willing to yield to the men, Mère Fanchette insists on entering before them. A dispute ensues between the two women during which they tear each other's hair and exchange coarse insults. When Jérôme warns them that the lord may drive them away for having soiled the premises with their fish that spilled in the course of the struggle, Mère Fanchette agrees to a compromise. Cadet will present the gifts of all assembled.

In *Les bottes de sept lieues,* Léandre wishes to carry off Isabelle from the house of her father Cassandre, who is opposed to their marriage. While Léandre bemoans Isabelle's destiny and declares his love for her, his servant Arlequin warns him of the arrival of Cassandre and his servant Gilles. Cassandre has just inherited twenty thousand écus and must be off to invest them. He instructs Gilles to keep watch over Isabelle and the money during his absence. Arlequin convinces Léandre that outwitting Gilles would enable them to get away with Isabelle and the money. Léandre and Arlequin appear in front of Gilles in a disguise. Arlequin introduces himself as Gilles's cousin. He informs him that his father has died and that his mother is dying. Gilles would like to return to his native village on hearing such news but cannot do so being under Cassandre's orders. Arlequin tells him that his master's "seven league boots" would enable him to make the trip back and forth before Cassandre's return. Arlequin helps Gilles on with the boots and, in the process, ties him up hand and foot. The projected escape becomes a reality. Léandre soon returns with Isabelle and tells Cassandre that he saved her from the hands of bandits who wanted to carry her off. As a reward, Léandre is allowed to marry Isabelle.

Jean Bête à la foire is probably a perfected version of a parade entitled *Léandre.*[2] Jean Bête is in love with Isabelle whom he would like to marry all the more quickly since she has already borne him two children and is pregnant with the third. Here again, Cassandre is opposed to their marriage. Jean Bête tells Arlequin of his narrow escape as he was recognized by Cassandre when trying to see Isabelle under the disguise of a doctor coming to treat her. Jean Bête is so desperate that he wishes to kill himself. Isabelle informs her father that she will do the same if she is not allowed to marry Jean Bête. The situation does not appear as tragic to Arlequin who advises his master to disguise himself as a bear-leader while he will play the role of the bear. Cassandre and his servant Gilles are, indeed, amused by them, while Jean Bête sees Isabelle again. Cassandre's watchfulness prevents Arlequin from carrying off Isabelle as planned. He returns under a new disguise and gets into a scuffle with Cassandre and Gilles, who come out of it wounded and needing the services of a doctor. The latter will be none other than Jean Bête who takes advantage of the situation to treat Isabelle as well. Ultimately,

Jean Bête reveals his identity as Jean Bête, the playwright. Cassandre gives his consent to the marriage, and the parade ends with a
compliment to Lenormand d'Etioles.

Although Beaumarchais never ascribed much importance to the
Parades, which were not published in full until 1956, they contribute
much to the understanding of all his plays. Jacques Schérer has
shown that they contain themes, situations, and stylistic forms that
reappear in the dramas as well as in the comedies.[3] *Colin et Colette*
is the scene of a lovers' quarrel, *dépit amoureux*, as we find them in
the dramas and the comedies. The theme of the bouquet reappears
in the *Mariage de Figaro*. In *Les bottes de sept lieues* and *Jean Bête
à la foire*, the plot rests on the element of disguise which plays an essential role in the comedies. Arlequin may be considered a first
sketch of Figaro, for he represents the mastermind of the plot, while
Jean Bête, like Figaro, is a playwright who seeks love and money and
criticizes the established order. Like Isabelle, Eugénie is pregnant, a
situation more tolerable in a parade than in a drama. Jean Bête refers
to his "grand-père paternel, maternel, fraternel, tanternel, sempiternel" (scene IX), while, in the *Barbier de Séville*, Almaviva, disguised as a drunken soldier, assumes that Bartholo is Rosine's
"bisaieul paternel, maternel, sempiternel" (II, 14). Finally, the
dramatic situations of the *Parades*, as simple as they may be, are
already derived from the psychology of the characters.

Lintilhac claims to have discovered an additional parade in which
he sees the first sketch of what was to become the *Barbier de
Séville*.[4] It resembles the other parades as it also presents a situation
where a young man wins a girl from the hands of her elderly guardian who intended to marry her himself. Léandre, Arlequin, and
Isabelle, or Zirzabelle, are again the names of the characters.
However, the name of the guardian is already Bartholo, who is being
counseled by Basile. Léandre is a count and Arlequin a barber, while
Isabelle's name is subsequently changed to that of Rosine. The
nature of such evidence has strengthened the theory that the *Barbier*
finds its origin in a parade as maintained by Jacques Schérer.[5]
However, since 1962, E. J. Arnould has repeatedly denied the existence of such a parade, claiming that Lintilhac has not sufficiently
substantiated his assertions.[6] Enzo Giudici subscribes to Lintilhac's
point of view concerning the link between the *Parades* and the *Barbier*.[7] Taking into account the disagreement between these two

scholars, Schérer has not found it necessary to modify his original view.[8]

II   *A Facetious Foreword*

The preface to the *Barbier* is entitled "Lettre modérée sur la chute et la critique du *Barbier de Séville*." The author writes in the subtitle that he is presenting his play to the reader "modestly dressed and bowing low." Beaumarchais allows himself such irony for, at the time he wrote the preface, the success of the play was assured. Although he points in it to the originality of his comedy, such critical analysis is not to be taken seriously, for it is drowned in many digressions which turn the preface into a piece of polemical writing.

Beaumarchais writes that he will speak of his play to the reader only if the latter has found full satisfaction with his appetite, his cook, and his mistress and feels thoroughly rested. Although he seeks the indulgence of the reader, he does not intend to flatter him as other authors do. Reviewing his past career as a playwright, Beaumarchais facetiously admits that his two dramas were "monstrous productions" for it is well known that no other genre exists besides tragedy and comedy. Characters struggling with the misfortunes of everyday life as shown in the drama are not understood. On the stage are allowed only unfortunate kings or ridiculous citizens. Should Beaumarchais venture to write another drama, he would make sure to devise for it a situation unrealistic enough to grant it instant success. He also regrets that his *Mémoires*, written under pressing circumstances, were not well received. Turning to his *Barbier*, Beaumarchais states that he elects the reader as its sole judge, since the critics think of it as a play without outline, plot, characters, unity, and void of comedy. Referring to the fiasco of the first performance and its ensuing success, Beaumarchais writes that, despite these so-called defects, "this poor Figaro . . . almost buried on Friday . . . resurrected on Sunday with a vigor that the austerity of an entire Lenten period and the weariness of seventeen public performances have not yet weakened."

Beaumarchais now undertakes to reply to his critics. He regrets their arrogance which little befits men of letters and makes it impossible for him to communicate with them. He insists that the theme of his play centered around an old lover supplanted by a younger one is not different from that of Molière's *L'Avare* or

Racine's *Mithridate*. He could even have turned it into a drama, had he chosen to follow the destiny of a Figaro born of a liaison between Bartholo and his maid Marceline. However, his intention was to create an amusing comedy where the bustling succession of events results from the confrontation between the joyful Figaro and Bartholo, the ever suspicious guardian of Rosine, who happens to be a bit less stupid than his stereotype in comedy.

Beaumarchais is particularly vexed with the critic of the *Journal de Bouillon* who has totally misunderstood the play. He states ironically that he is willing to forgive him for failing to see the beautiful comic scenes, which Beaumarchais purposely enumerates in detail. He will not forgive him for not discerning Figaro's filial devotion to his mother, in reality a trivial allusion in the play. The critic is again in error when he sees in Rosine an ill-bred person, and Beaumarchais wonders whether it would have made better sense for her to marry "the gouty old doctor" rather than a charming young lover. As for the pleasure felt by the critic seeing a whole act of the play eliminated before the second performance, Beaumarchais states that he has by no means violated the principles of theater on that matter, having originally composed the *Barbier* in five acts. If the critic of the *Journal de Bouillon* remains unhappy, it is because he does not find "merry things serious enough, nor serious things merry enough."

Beaumarchais ends the preface by replying to sundry criticisms. To those who reproach him for having allowed Bartholo to speak ill of French mores, he says that he originally intended to write the play in Spanish but finally decided to write it in French for the benefit of Parisian audiences. Concerning the resemblance between the *Barbier* and a play entitled *You can't think of everything*, Beaumarchais says that his comedy is that very play since no one ever thought of writing one like it. As for the man who noticed the resemblance, it is evident that he does not care to think much about anything. Those who think that Beaumarchais insulted women and doctors in his play lack a sense of humor, for they fail to see that he meant to amuse rather than offend. Finally, Beaumarchais explains that the *Barbier* did not remain an opera for, in that form, the music would have slowed up the development of comedy.

Some of the assertions made by Beaumarchais in the preface are inaccurate. It is known that his comedy had originally been composed in four acts and subsequently increased to five. Reducing it to four was merely restoring it to its original form. Not all the critics were as ill-disposed toward the *Barbier* as he maintains, and many had shown the appreciation it deserved.[9] It is because, as a comic opera, it had been refused by the *comédie italienne* that Beaumarchais, following the advice of his friends,[10] turned it into a comedy, and not for the theoretical reason he states. Yet, by taking to task the critic of the *Journal de Bouillon*, Beaumarchais gave himself the opportunity to extol his own gifts as a comic author. The *Lettre modérée* remains, therefore, another testimony of Beaumarchais's wit and introduces us to the gay atmosphere of the play.

IV   Le Barbier de Séville
ou La Précaution inutile

The useless precaution taken by a suspicious guardian who tries to keep his young ward from marrying the one she loves is a common theme that goes back to the comedy of Plautus. In the flourishing age of comedy, for which the seventeenth and eighteenth century are known, such a theme had gained widespread popularity. The subtitle of Beaumarchais's play is that of a short story by Scarron, which had already inspired Molière in plays such as *L'Ecole des femmes, L'Ecole des maris, L'Avare,* and many others. In his play *Les Folies amoureuses,* Regnard also showed an old guardian trying unsuccessfully to keep his ward in confinement. In the same play, the servant Crispin may have served as a model for Figaro as did the Crispin of Lesage's *Crispin rival de son maître.* The theme of the useless precaution recurs in *Le Remède à la mode,* a parade of disputed authorship, and obviously in *La Précaution inutile* by Nolan de Fatouville. Therefore, the originality of the *Barbier* should not be sought in the choice of the theme but rather in its dramatic technique and in the originality of its characters.

The transformations of the *Barbier de Séville* have been studied by Lintilhac.[11] He shows that following its first stage as a parade, it had become an *opéra-comique* in which the sentimentality of the lovers was too verbose and in which Bartholo, disguised as a monk, was more superstitious and less shrewd than in his final form. Beaumarchais transformed the opéra-comique into a four-act comedy lengthened into five acts between 1774 and 1775. Some of the additions contained in this last version alluded to his misfortunes as an author, to his trials, and to his adventures as a secret agent and were not directly relevant to the plot. Other additions were more amusing and indicative of Beaumarchais's Gallic spirit. However, many scenes were excessively long and caused the play to be highly unsuccessful in its first performance. For the subsequent performances, Beaumarchais reverted to the original four-act comedy which retained a few of the later additions and represents the final form of the play.[12]

Count Almaviva sets about to learn the identity of the beautiful young girl he once noticed in Madrid. Having discovered that her name is Rosine and that she lives with the old Bartholo in Séville, he has come there and waits for her to appear at her window. He is aware of the senselessness of his pursuit, especially when the Court at Madrid offers him much easier conquests. He realizes, however, that these are chiefly motivated by intrigue, greed, and vanity, whereas he seeks the happiness of being loved for himself.

Almaviva's dream would have been scarcely realized had he not met by chance his former servant Figaro, who happens to be employed by Bartholo as barber, surgeon, and apothecary. Figaro tells his former master that he was dismissed from the job for which Almaviva had recommended him when it was learned that he was an author. He is now convinced that "the useful revenue of the razor is preferable to the fruitless honor of the pen." Therefore, he goes about "mocking the fools and defying the wicked, laughing off misery and bearding everybody"(I,3), and declares himself ready to serve his former master again.

As they are both conversing, the jalousie opens and Bartholo appears at the window with Rosine. He is disgruntled with her for studying the couplets of *The Useless Precaution*, which he considers one of the many senseless productions of a barbarous age. Rosine drops into the street the sheet of paper which is nothing else but a message to the count requesting him to identify himself in a song. Then, she asks Bartholo to fetch the paper, and, while he goes down into the street, she motions to the count to pick it up. Almaviva immediately obeys her orders, and when the suspicious Bartholo returns empty-handed and angry, he locks the jalousie with a key vowing that such a situation will not repeat itself.

To Bartholo's suspicion there is but one remedy, namely, to marry

Rosine as soon as possible. To this end, he has despatched Bazile, Rosine's singing teacher and his man of confidence, to a notary, instructing him to arrange the marriage for the next day. Almaviva soon realizes that romantic lovemaking will not get him far, and he becomes increasingly dependent on Figaro's cunning in his endeavor to approach Rosine. Figaro informs him that a real strategy is to be planned to overcome Bartholo's suspicion. At first, he thinks of diverting the attention of the guards by drugging them. As this project may prove too risky, he proposes that Almaviva disguise himself as a drunken soldier requesting lodgings in Bartholo's house. As Rosine appears at her window, Figaro urges the count to identify himself in a song according to her instructions. Accompanying himself with Figaro's guitar, the count says that he is known as Lindor. He confides to his servant that by using that pseudonym he is reserving for himself a delightful triumph, which he will enjoy when he reveals to Rosine that he is really Count Almaviva. When she acknowledges his reply, he is overjoyed. Figaro overwhelmingly espouses the cause of his master, and he exclaims: "As for me, I'll go in here and use all the tricks of my trade in one master stroke, to disarm vigilance, awaken love, mislead jealousy, baffle schemes, and overcome all obstacles. You, Sir, at my house in a soldier's uniform, with an order for lodging and money in your pockets" (I, 6).

Rosine is solely preoccupied by her curiosity about Lindor. Surreptitiously, she writes him a letter, although she does not even know by what means she could send it to him. She decides to question Figaro, who has succeeded in entering the house by drugging the guards, about Lindor. The servant presents his master as a handsome, promising, witty, sensitive, and talented young man who, nevertheless, "has one serious fault," that of being in love. To Rosine this is far from being a fault, and she asks who is the person with whom Lindor is in love. As a reply, Figaro presents another portrait and asks Rosine to imagine "the prettiest little darling, sweet, tender, gentle, so fresh you want to eat her up; nimble feet, supple waist, slender, with round arms, a rosy mouth, and such hands! such cheeks! such teeth! such eyes!" Rosine's curiosity is now irrepressibly aroused, and Figaro admits that the person is none other than Bartholo's ward. Filled with emotion, Rosine asks Figaro to instruct Lindor to remain absolutely still. Whereupon Figaro explains to Rosine that, inasmuch as youth has to make the "terrible choice between love without repose, or repose without love," the former "looks a little more attractive." Rosine then hands Figaro the letter she has just written informing him that her friendship is motivated by pure friendship only. Figaro explains that Lindor's feelings are of a quite different nature. Describing them he says: "When he merely speaks of his love, he breathes such fire that I almost burn with passion, and I am only a bystander" (II, 2).

At this point, Bartholo enters angrily, scarcely giving Figaro time to hide in an adjoining room. He rails against Figaro, who has given sleeping pills to L'Eveillé ("The Awakened One"), has turned La Jeunesse ("The Youthful One") into a limping and sneezing man, has bled Marceline's foot, and applied a cataplasm on the mule's eyes. Bartholo supposes that by means of such services, Figaro wishes to repay him the rent of a hundred écus he owes him. Yet, the consequences of this situation are disastrous, for, owing to the incapacitated servants, the house is open to anyone. He declares himself all the more concerned that the paper dropped by Rosine into the street has never been found. He informs her of his intention to nail down the shutter altogether, for his suspicion is now cast on Figaro himself. In a desperate outburst, Rosine tells him that he may wall up the windows as well, and she admits that she has indeed spoken with Figaro whom she finds very pleasant.

To Bartholo, only Bazile is trustworthy. Indeed, Bazile arrives with the news that Count Almaviva has come to Séville in a disguise in order to seek Rosine. Bartholo tells him that he would not be reluctant to have the count killed in an ambush. Bazile believes that for a man of the count's stature slander is a more powerful weapon. At this point, Bazile recites the "calumny tirade," an allusion to Beaumarchais's adventures, which are rather irrelevant to the plot. Bartholo dismisses this suggestion as nonsense and prefers to renew his instructions to Bazile concerning the marriage. As Bartholo sees him to the door, Figaro, who has overheard the conversation, comes out of hiding. Before escaping, he informs Rosine of Bartholo's intention to marry her but assures her that everything will be done in order to divert him from it.

Bartholo's suspiciousness is further put to the test when he rightly guesses that Figaro is serving as some kind of intermediary between Rosine and some lover. As for Rosine, she can hardly believe that her guardian has such an unmistakable instinct of jealousy. To deny his accurate charge that she has just written a letter, she must resort to lying, while he remains skeptical about her contrived explanations. He is wary again when he faces the count disguised as a drunken soldier requesting lodging, for Almaviva has indeed set before himself the difficult task of handing a letter to Rosine under the very eyes of her guardian. Despite the count's efforts at concealing the letter, at substituting for it other documents, at diverting Bartholo's attention by insulting him, none of the count's moves has escaped Bartholo. As Almaviva, who has succeeded in leaving the letter with Rosine, is finally dismissed, the guardian violently wrenches it out of his ward's pocket. Simulating a fainting spell, Rosine shrewdly submits to his will for she has succeeded in substituting for the count's letter one she has received from her cousin.

The count, disguised as a student, once again enters Bartholo's house. He hopes to inform Rosine of his plans to prevent Bartholo from marrying her. To avoid dismissal, the count introduces himself as Alonzo, the pupil of Bazile, who was unable to come himself due to illness. On hearing such news, Bartholo is ready to visit his man of confidence in the company of the student with whom he is ready to leave at once. The count must quickly think of a way to gain time, and decides to tell Bartholo in the name of Bazile that he has learned that Almaviva has written to Rosine. Such artifice does not fail to produce a shift in the guardian's attitude, and he suddenly asks the count to speak more softly, whereas he had bid him previously to speak louder, pretending to be deaf in one ear. At this point, the scene is punctuated by Bartholo's appeals to the count to speak more softly, as the latter persists in speaking loudly. To retain Bartholo's confidence, the count has no other choice but to show him the letter he received from Rosine. The count suggests that confronting Rosine with this proof of her betrayal would undoubtedly hasten the guardian's marriage. Delighted, Bartholo retains the letter, much to the count's displeasure, and proposes that the count meet Rosine so that the confrontation they have just devised may not appear too contrived. Bartholo will introduce the count as a music teacher who has come instead of Bazile.

As pointed out by Jacques Schérer, a sequence of unexpected happenings (péripéties-éclairs), each of which annuls the former, heightens the comic tension.[13] The count is delighted at the prospect of seeing Rosine. However, she refuses to take a music lesson, as

proposed by Bartholo, for she is angry at him because of the letter incident. Yet, having noticed the presence of the count, she feels a
slight discomfort as a result of her surprise and changes her mind.
Now, it is Bartholo who wishes to postpone the music lesson for fear
of indisposing her further. However, the count advises him not to
antagonize her, and the music lesson will take place as planned.
Rosine sings a song concerning a shepherdess who longs for her lover
named Lindor, while Bartholo, having insisted on being present during the lesson, finds that song too *romanesque* and suggests one that
concerns an elderly man courting a young girl.

The music lesson affords the lovers the opportunity to gain time.
Yet, the count, who has barely communicated with Rosine, can act
no further and must rely upon Figaro's ingeniousness. As he arrives,
he claims that he has come to give Bartholo a shave, intending to
draw him away in another room to find the necessary utensils. After
haggling back and forth, Figaro succeeds in his scheme and, in the
process, gains possession of the key to the jalousie of Bartholo's
house. However, the guardian's absence is brief. It allows the count
time to inform Rosine that he intends to be back in the evening but
not to explain to her his reasons for having handed over her letter to
Bartholo.

The famous "stupefaction scene" takes place with the untimely
arrival of Bazile who represents a danger to all assembled, since he
may deny the existence of Alonzo. The scene can be divided into five
movements during which Bazile goes from one amazement to
another. Each of these movements is dominated by a leitmotiv. The
first is that of "Alonzo" of whom Bazile has never heard. The second
is the command "keep quiet" addressed to Bazile by everyone the
moment he attempts to speak. The third is the repetition of the word
"lawyer" in relation to the marriage arrangements on which Bazile
is to report to Bartholo, who is eager to learn about their progress.
However, the count quickly convinces Bartholo to drop the subject
in the presence of Rosine. The fourth is the command "go to sleep"
addressed to Bazile, along with the suggestion that he is not at all
well. When he finally agrees to leave after the count has surreptitiously slipped a purse in his hands, everyone bids him "good
night," and he replies with the same greeting utterly
amazed.

Figaro now proceeds with the shaving of Bartholo. However, the guardian insists upon witnessing the continuation of the music lesson since he cannot help harboring some suspicion about leaving Rosine and her music teacher to themselves. Figaro's ingeniousness gives rise to a new sequence of péripéties-éclairs. Tying the towel around Bartholo's neck, Figaro causes his view to be obstructed. However, the guardian insists on observing the couple. Figaro, then, gives a shriek, pretending that something has entered his eye. Lowering his head toward that of Bartholo, Figaro asks him to look into his eye, thus obstructing his view once more. Bartholo, then, pushes him away violently and walks over to the couple. Indeed, the count was in the process of informing Rosine that being in the possession of the key to the jalousie, he and Figaro would return in the evening. The count was about to explain to her that due to his useless disguise he was forced to show her letter to Bartholo, who retained it. However, such explanation does not take place. Hearing the count mention a "useless disguise," Bartholo unmasks him forthwith, calling him "perfidious Alonzo." Leaving the guardian fuming with anger and Rosine in rebellion against him, the count and Figaro make their way out with the leitmotiv "out of his mind" addressed to Bartholo. In a brief monologue, Bartholo is somewhat tragic as he curses his tormentors and realizes in despair that there is no one to help him.

Bazile now informs Bartholo that the notary cannot arrive before four o'clock in the morning, as he has been retained to perform the marriage of Figaro's niece at Figaro's house. Knowing that such a niece does not exist, Bartholo's suspicion about Figaro is now confirmed. Alarmed at the thought of losing Rosine, Bartholo orders Bazile to bring the notary without delay, and, to speed matters, he hands him the passkey to the house. Meanwhile, the guardian confronts his ward with her own letter written to the count. Convinced that she has been betrayed, Rosine surrenders to her fate, and, in her despair, declares her willingness to marry Bartholo. To avenge herself, she informs him that Figaro and the count are to be back in the evening entering through the jalousie of which they possess the key. Satisfied and forewarned, Bartholo goes off to prepare an ambush to overtake his foes.

The count and Figaro have penetrated into Bartholo's house to take away Rosine. In view of Bartholo's revelations, she meets the count's enthusiasm with the cool pride of an abandoned mistress.

This temporary obstacle is the occasion for a typical scene of an amorous quarrel during which the count becomes aware that he is loved for himself. Throwing off his mantle, he appears in a magnificent dress and identifies himself as Count Almaviva. This unexpected revelation causes Rosine to faint, and this fainting fit is nothing else but an expression of love as realized by Figaro who exclaims: "My word, how beautiful she is" (IV, 7).

The count and Figaro cannot escape with Rosine as planned, since the ladder they used to penetrate into the house through the jalousie has been taken away. Arriving with the notary, Bazile does not understand why Bartholo has given him the passkey to the house, where he finds the count, Figaro, and Rosine assembled. The notary is perplexed as well when he realizes that in the same evening he is to perform two marriages where both brides are named Rosine. These difficulties are overlooked as the count urges the notary to perform the marriage and Bazile to sign as witness, which he agrees to do thanks to a purse that the count slips into his hands. When the alcalde and policemen, eventually brought in by Bartholo to arrest the count, become aware of the entire situation, they do not carry out their mission. As Bartholo reproaches himself with having been too careless, Figaro asks him to meditate rather upon the following truth: ". . . when youth and love conspire together to deceive an old man, anything he might do to stop them may well be called *The Useless Precaution*" (IV, 8).

The Barbier de Séville is followed by a *Compliment de clôture* or closing sketch. Usually played at the end of a theatrical season, such a sketch was to flatter the public, express the humility of the actors, and announced the titles of plays to be presented during the forthcoming season. The *Barbier's* compliment is an amusing and witty playlet in which the characters of the comedy reappear. Bartholo is seen perplexed about composing the compliment, Rosine wishes to sing it, the count announces the forthcoming titles and speaks of the humility of the actors, Bazile is once again sent to bed, and Figaro affirms the usefulness of the box-office returns that compensate the actors. There are two versions of the *Compliment de clôture*. The first was intended to be played at the closing of the theatrical season of 1775 but, in all probability, was never presented among other reasons, because of the rift that existed between Beaumarchais and the actors of the Comédie-Française over the

settlement of his account. The second version was presented
between 1791 and 1793 at the Théâtre du Marais, where the *Barbier*
was being performed.

Beaumarchais wrote that *Le Barbier de Séville* is a true expression
of his gay character and that, in composing it, he merely brought
back good old gaiety to the stage. With a common theme and
stereotyped characters, he created a comedy that goes beyond the
imitations of Molière as they were practiced in the eighteenth century. In the *Barbier*, the personalities of the characters, the accumulation of comic situations, and the style are artfully combined
to generate laughter.

It was pointed out that Bartholo was tragic when he realizes that
he has been betrayed. Such despair, however, is but a moment of his
behavior that remains utterly comic throughout the play owing to
his excessive suspiciousness. Yet, even such suspiciousness cannot be
consistently maintained by him if the action is to progress, and it is
for this reason that Beaumarchais has allowed him to weaken on certain occasions. Thus, one may wonder why the guardian's eye does
not catch Rosine substituting the letter of her cousin for that of the
count, why he does not recognize the count disguised as a student
shortly after he has seen him in the disguise of a drunken soldier,
why he is allowed to fall asleep during the music lesson thus enabling the count to kiss Rosine's arm, or why he does not catch Figaro
and the count before they can enter the house through the jalousie.
Such oversights cause Bartholo to be the architect of his own downfall, which is another comic dimension of this character. He even
goes so far as to unknowingly utter the truth when he tells the count
disguised as Alonzo, "You look more like a lover in disguise than an
accomplice" (III, 2).

Almaviva lends himself to the various tricks suggested or prepared
by Figaro which will bring him face to face with Rosine in the un-
wanted presence of her guardian. On these occasions, Almaviva is
comic for he continues Figaro's work thanks to his own flashes of
wit. In his simulated drunkeness, he plays on the guardian's name
and insults him. Bartholo is in turn "Balordo," "Barque à l'eau,"
"Barbe à l'eau," and "Barbaro." When the guardian claims that
Rosine is his wife, the count replies, "I took you for her grandfather,
paternal, maternal, sempiternal" (II, 14). It is thanks to Almaviva's
interventions that Bartholo participates in the "stupefaction" of

Bazile, and it is thanks to his purses of money slipped into Bazile's hands at the right moment that the latter is kept from ruining his scheme. Once Almaviva's success is assured, he discards his comic masks and becomes again the sentimental lover who relishes the bliss of being loved for himself.

For a brief moment, Figaro, who has been rightfully hailed as the "machinist" of the play, stumbles upon one of the obstacles placed in his way by Bartholo. To justify the absence of a sheet of paper that was used to write to Lindor, Rosine told her guardian that she wrapped in it some sweets intended for Figaro's daughter (II, 11). Later, when Bartholo takes Figaro to task and wishes to know if his little girl liked the sweets, the servant is suddenly taken aback, for Rosine never informed him of Bartholo's investigation. It is only when she intervenes with a pseudo-reminder concerning the sweets that Figaro is able to say that his little daughter liked them fine (III, 5). This momentary vacillation on the part of Figaro is not only comic but introduces a realistic note in his ruse, which might have appeared contrived otherwise.

To all other charges brought against him by Bartholo, Figaro replies instantaneously. When he is asked what he will say to L'Eveillé who yawns and to La Jeunesse who sneezes, he answers, "Oh, well, to the one who sneezes I'll say, 'God bless you,' and 'Go to bed' to the one who yawns." Upon being reminded about the hundred écus he owes Bartholo, he rejoins, "Your hundred écus! I would rather owe them to you for a lifetime than deny them to you for a single moment" (III, 5). Neither is Figaro afraid to rebuke the count if the occasion calls for it. When Almaviva reminds him of his faults, he retorts, "If you judge masters by the virtues you expect in their servants, does Your Excellency know many who are worthy of being valets?" (I, 2). He also proves to be a man of feeling as he makes himself the advocate of the count's love or as he witnesses the triumph of that love. A self-made man who has once been an author, Figaro goes beyond the typical *valet de comédie*. Having an acute sense of reality, he is willing to serve his former master's design not so much because of the reward promised, but because he wishes to defend the order of nature against those who intend to disturb it.[14]

Rosine's attitude is far from passive in the midst of the rivalry that opposes her guardian to the Count and Figaro. She awakens our compassion as she laments her destiny, but her situation has made her aware of the necessity of shrewdness. After she has successfully deceived her guardian in the episode of the extorted letter, she justifies her behavior by observing, ". . . an unjust man would make a schemer out of innocence itself" (II, 16). From that moment on, she will not miss an opportunity to become a party to the plots that are planned to undo Bartholo's project of marrying her. She also demonstrates feminine cleverness as she waits for Figaro to spell out that she herself is the object of the count's pursuit (II, 2). As a woman in love, she shows haughty indignation when she thinks that she has been betrayed but instantaneously surrenders to the count's love upon realizing that it is genuine.

In serving his master, Bazile is solely motivated by greed. When Bartholo rebukes him at the outset for not carrying out his orders with enough zeal, he replies: "Yes, but you've skimped on the expenses. In the harmony of a well-ordered society, an unequal marriage, a crooked verdict, an obvious injustice are discords which should always be prepared and resolved by the perfect concord of gold." When Bartholo reluctantly gives him additional money, he says: "That's the way to talk. Tomorrow everything will be over" (II, 8). However, in the course of the day, the count has outbidden the guardian. All Bazile can say when Bartholo rebukes him once more at the end of the play is: "This devil of a man [the count] always has his pockets full of irresistible arguments" (IV, 8).

As shown by its various transformations, *Le Barbier de Séville* represents a perfected form of the comic art that Beaumarchais had been cultivating since he wrote the *Parades*. The final form of this comedy reveals his ability to construct a complex but solid intrigue, to enliven old comic types, and to endow his characters with a sparkling language. Beaumarchais's preface to the *Barbier* should be seen solely as his awareness of his own success. Yet, he seems to remain unsatisfied by this achievement, for he seeks to further complicate intrigue and intensify gaiety. It is such ambitions that will bring about the existence of the *Mariage de Figaro*.

CHAPTER 5

Sparkling Gaiety

T HE overwhelming success which greeted the *Mariage de Figaro* when it was finally presented on the French stage should be viewed as an accurate appraisal of Beaumarchais's dramatic genius. One of the longest plays of the French theater, it is also one of the most complex. In composing it, Beaumarchais not only devised a complicated intrigue but he exposed the mores of his times, designed types, introduced emotional episodes, and raised social and political issues. All these elements are combined to create an eventful action which takes place in a single "mad day," which is the subtitle of the play. In dealing with such a diversity of genres, Beaumarchais could not avoid many scenes, events, and tirades that prove to be extraneous to the main action. Yet, he succeeded in creating an atmosphere of sparkling gaiety which gives the play both unity and originality. Our concern here is to elucidate the complicated plot, to evaluate the characters, and to reassess the multiple significance of Beaumarchais's masterpiece.

I *The Preface*

After the *Mariage* had been performed for nearly a year, Beaumarchais wrote a preface to defend the morality of his play. He writes that the function of theater is to correct vices. Failure to view it in such perspective could result in draining the repertoire of the great classic masterpieces as well as in restraining the talent of the actors. Beaumarchais asserts that his play has a corrective intent thereby hoping to put an end to the degradation of the theater.

Beaumarchais then reviews his career as a playwright from the point of view of morality. If *Eugénie* was well received, it is because he had the courage to depict the baseness of a man who uses his reputation to seduce a helpless young woman. *Les Deux Amis* also teaches a moral lesson insofar as it shows a father who is sincere

enough to admit to his so-called niece that she is actually his illegitimate daughter. Although "frank gaiety" is restored with the
Barbier de Séville, people tell Beaumarchais: "Why don't you write
more such plays since you are the only one who dares to laugh off
vices with frankness."

Le Mariage de Figaro does not violate ethics in any of its aspects.
Beaumarchais is certain that critics would have received it better had
it been some grave drama. Yet, its gentle intrigue conceals a
profound morality under its joyful atmosphere. None of the
characters can be said to behave immorally. Count Almaviva is
shown constantly frustrated in his plans to seduce women. The
countess outwits her husband only to make him more aware of his
marital duties. Even if she does not remain indifferent toward the
affection shown to her by Chérubin, she retains her dignity by
mastering her feelings. As the target of the count's pursuit, Suzanne
acts with a clear conscience as she warns her future husband Figaro
and the countess, who might have become victims of the situation
otherwise, of the count's intentions. Figaro cannot be regarded as
dishonest when circumstances force him to use all his cunning in
order to rescue his happiness. Neither can Chérubin be condemned
for repeatedly expressing his affection for the countess, as he is still a
child. In fact, his presence in the play constantly serves to remind
the count of his guilt. Marceline may seem immoral as a result of her
former liaison with Bartholo of which Figaro was born. Yet, she
greatly redeems herself by reminding the audience that she yielded
in a moment of weakness and by warning helpless women against
vile seducers.

Beaumarchais claims that he never intended to criticize the established order. In portraying a frivolous nobleman, he did not mean
to satirize the aristocracy as a whole, for which he always had high
regard, but rather the individual who damages his reputation as an
aristocrat. He explains that when Figaro says: "To accept, to take,
and to demand—there is the courtier's secret in three words," he
means to define solely the unscrupulous courtier. Through the
character of Brid'oison, Beaumarchais did not wish to attack judges
in general but only those who abuse their power as representatives of
justice. Nor did he intend to attack the military when Figaro says

82 BEAUMARCHAIS

that he does not want to resemble a blindly obedient soldier. All he meant was that man should be able to enjoy his freedom. By having the countess say that she wishes to end her life at the convent of the "Ursulines," Beaumarchais did not wish to deride that particular religious order, since the choice of the name was a pure matter of chance. As for Figaro's monologue, even it it contains some daring truths concerning men who exert power, it should by no means raise concern, for, according to Beaumarchais, the king and his political regime are enlightened enough to allow the criticism of genuine oppressors.

The preface also contains some remarks about the art of the play. Beaumarchais asserts that its style is deliberately diversified as each character speaks in his own manner under particular circumstances. Beaumarchais praises its unfailing gaiety, its lively dialogue, its smooth intrigue "whose art conceals its artfulness, which tangles and untangles unceasingly through a host of comic situations and of piquant and varied tableaux, which sustain without fatiguing the attention of the audience during the three and a half hours the spectacle consumes (an attempt that no man of letters ever made before). . . ." Finally, Beaumarchais extols the universality of the play which depicts in no way the mores of his day but rather those of former and future times.

II *Some Possible Influences on Le Mariage de Figaro*

As Beaumarchais's comedy deals with a variety of themes, one can only mention some of the works which may have influenced it. On the theme of the lord's right to the first wedding night, Voltaire had written a play entitled *Le Droit du seigneur* (1762). In *La Précaution inutile*, Scarron had written the story of a duchess who hides a lover into a closet and arranges his escape after she has overcome her husband's jealousy. This theme which was very popular in the eighteenth century is also the subject of *La Gageure imprévue* (1768), a one-act play by Sedaine. The lonely wife who is about to yield to a younger lover is the subject of several plays in the eighteenth century. One of them is *Heureusement* (1762) by Rochon de Chabannes, which Beaumarchais explicitly mentions in his preface as a source of his comedy. The satire of judges and justice goes back to the comedy of Aristophanes. It is the subject of Racine's *Les Plaideurs*. In the *Mariage*, judge Brid'oison recalls judge Bridoie

Enters Chérubin, the count's page. He seeks Suzanne's sympathy over his dismissal from the castle ordered by the count, who dis- in Rabelais's *Tiers-Livre*. A husband making love to his disguised wife whom he believes to be the girl he pursues is a widespread comic device in eighteenth-century comedy. It is the subject of Dufresny's *Double Veuvage* (1702) and Vadé's *Trompeur trompé* (1754). Chérubin, one of the most original characters of the play, resembles the hero of *Le Petit Jehan de Saintré* (1517), a novel by Antoine de La Salle re-edited by Gueullette in 1724. On the other hand, in creating Chérubin, Beaumarchais may have been inspired by observing his own environment, especially Petit-Louis or "cher Lubin", a young page and musician who woos the duchess of Choiseul, who is neglected by her husband.[1] The above review il- lustrates the literary background of the *Mariage* but does not ac- count in any way for Beaumarchais's power of imagination in com- posing it.

III *The First Act*

At the castle of Aguas-Frescas, Figaro, the servant of Count Almaviva, is in love with Suzanne, the countess' chambermaid, and is about to marry her in the course of the day. Figaro learns from his fiancée that he must not consider himself a joyful groom. Indeed, Bazile, the agent of the count's pleasures, has informed her that the count seeks to obtain from her the lord's privilege of the first night for which he is willing to compensate by a dowry. Suzanne feels that there is no time for lovemaking until Figaro meets such a challenge. Although he knows that thwarting the count's desires is no easy matter, he realizes that quick action is imperative. Invigorated by his love, Figaro decides upon his plans for the day. He will set an earlier hour for the marriage ceremony to make sure that it will take place, ward off Marceline, who is too fond of him, get all the money and presents in his hands, and give Bazile a good thrashing.

A rivalry exists between Marceline and Suzanne over Figaro. Marceline wishes him to fulfill a marriage commitment he made to her for failure to pay her a debt. To this end, she has asked Bartholo, her former lover, to help her win the servant. As for herself, she will spread the rumor concerning the count's pursuit of Suzanne, expec- ting the latter to refuse the count's advances as she wishes to main- tain an honorable reputation. Consequently, the count will oppose

Suzanne's marriage to Figaro out of frustration and favor
Marceline's.
covered him in the room of Fanchette, the daughter of the gardener
Antonio, who happens to be Suzanne's uncle. An adolescent
awakening to love, Chérubin is not content with Fanchette but also
courts Suzanne and even Marceline. Above all, he has come to tell
Suzanne that he is fond of the countess whom he finds noble and
beautiful but "so distant" (I, 7). As observed by Guy Michaud, we
have here an intrigue where Chérubin is three times the rival of the
count, who, while pursuing Fanchette and Suzanne, has by no
means renounced his wife.[2] Failing to approach the countess,
Chérubin takes from Suzanne a ribbon belonging to her mistress. As
Suzanne tries to retrieve it, the count enters leaving both Suzanne
and Chérubin stricken with fright. All the page has time to do is hide
in back of a big armchair, which is the only piece of furniture in the
room.

Almaviva is more than pleased to find Suzanne alone. He mentions to her the matter of the *droit du seigneur* which he would like
to discuss with her later in the evening. This is the famous and lively
"armchair scene." In order to hide Chérubin better, Suzanne has
placed herself between him and the count. As they are conversing,
Bazile enters. The count, who does not wish to be seen speaking with
Suzanne, seeks a hiding place and does not find a better one than
behind the armchair. While he is about to place himself there,
Chérubin turns about and throws himself into the armchair in a
curled-up position. Thereupon, Suzanne covers him with one of the
countess' dresses she is carrying. As pointed out by Jacques Schérer,
the performance of all these actions in a matter of seconds is a
brilliant experiment in theatrical physics. If the stage is the "first
location," Chérubin has moved into a "third location" from a second one now occupied by the count.[3] Furthermore, as pointed out
by Guy Michaud, the count is forced into a ridiculous and hence
comic position, because he is obliged to hide.[4]

Comic tension is further heightened in the scene when Bazile
speaks of the count's intention to an indignant Suzanne. He suggests
that she submit to the count all the more since she is also being pursued by the page, who, besides, publicizes his love for the countess.
Upon hearing such news related by Bazile, the count jumps to his
feet and orders the definite dismissal of the page. Almaviva takes the

opportunity to tell Suzanne how he discovered Chérubin hidden behind a curtain in Fanchette's room. Reenacting the scene for Suzanne, he lifts the dress off the armchair thereby finding himself once again face to face with the page. Suzanne explains that Chérubin had come to ask her to intervene with the countess on his behalf. In so doing, she is forced to enlighten the count on the movements around the armchair. To conceal his embarrassment, the count asserts himself by declaring that he cannot allow Figaro to marry Suzanne, who is evidently unfaithful.

The count is unable to take this last decision seriously, because he is met by his entire household and the people of his jurisdiction who, under the leadership of Figaro, have gathered to ask him for the official abolition of the droit du seigneur. As their request is being wholeheartedly supported by the countess, the count must yield to the pressure. Although this is one of Figaro's victories, the count still hopes to hinder his marriage to Suzanne by substituting Marceline for her. It is under the same pressure that the count is asked to forgive Chérubin. Almaviva yields again but is not wholly defeated as his pardon consists of granting the page an officer's commission that will estrange him from the castle just as well. Figaro understands this and outwits the count by instructing the page to ostensibly leave the castle on horseback but to return on foot through the back way.

IV   *The Second Act*

In the words of Jean Meyer, the second act "is the perfect act, a one-act play in itself."[5] The decor here is essential. It consists of a splendid bedroom, with a large bed in an alcove, an entry door on the right, the door of a closet at left, a door at the back, and a window.

Suzanne's revelations make the countess aware of Chérubin's feeling toward her and of the extent to which she is being neglected by the count. Giving way to emotion, she reproaches herself for having wearied her husband with her love. On the other hand, she wishes to see her maid's marriage come about and will cooperate with Figaro to this end. He soon arrives with a plan that he outlines to the two women. First, he announces that he has given to Bazile an anonymous note warning the count that a gallant wishes to see the countess during the ball that is to take place in the evening. Secondly, he enjoins Suzanne to accept the private meeting sought by the count, since he will substitute for her Chérubin disguised as a girl. Although the countess realizes that the initiative taken by Figaro is damaging to her reputation, she is willing to support the plan, for Suzanne declares that "one may rely upon him to conduct an intrigue" (II, 2).

The arrival of Chérubin is a pleasant interlude for the sad countess who is tacitly delighted to see herself as the object of his admiration. Prompted by Suzanne, he bashfully sings a medieval romance in which a page grieves over the loss of his godmother, a situation akin to his. In a sequence of short scenes penetrated with a delicate sensuality, the women are seen fussing over the page's feminine disguise. As the countess discovers the stolen ribbon on his arm, she retrieves it and orders Suzanne to replace it with another one. Thus, she is discreetly in possession of a token of the page's love.

The soothing calmness of this atmosphere is troubled by the unexpected arrival of the count, who knocks on the door of the bedroom. While Suzanne is busy in a back room, Chérubin and the countess are stricken with fright. While the countess tarries in opening the door, the page throws himself into the closet of which she retains the key. The count tells his wife about the note that was handed to him by Bazile. She calms his fears by informing him that she has no intention of leaving the room for the rest of the day due to some indisposition. But when Chérubin knocks over a chair in the closet, the count's suspicion is rekindled, and he demands to examine its interior. In this highly tense moment, the countess has no alternative but to lie. She says that the closet cannot be opened because Suzanne is standing in it half-dressed. Realizing that it would be useless to ask his wife for the key to the closet, the count decides to fetch the necessary tools to break it open. To make sure that no one will enter or leave the room in his absence, he locks its back and entry doors and requests his wife to accompany him. In the course of that scene, Suzanne has reentered the bedroom through the back door and, upon witnessing the situation, has time to throw herself into the alcove unseen by the count. The departure of the count and countess enables her to substitute herself in the closet for Chérubin, who has barely time to jump through the window.[6]

In view of the count's firmness, the countess must admit what she believes to be the truth at the time, namely, that Chérubin is in the closet. Angered by the recurring presence of the page, the count threatens to kill him. Such furor brings the countess down to her knees as she intercedes for the life of Chérubin. Then, she gives the key to the closet to the count, who, upon opening it, finds Suzanne walking out of it laughing.[7] The count can only marvel at his wife's capacity to feign emotion and distress. He tries to apologize for his outburst by explaining to her that the note he received from Bazile had greatly disturbed him. Relieved at the happy outcome of such a dangerous situation, the countess, in a moment of thoughtlessness, admits to her husband that it was Figaro who handed the note to Bazile. In any case, the count is intent upon being pardoned by his wife, and it is his turn to beg for forgiveness.

With the arrival of Figaro, the dramatic tension heightens again. Ignoring the previous sequence of events, he is at a loss when the count asks him to explain the origins of Bazile's note. He tries to wrangle himself out of this embarrassing situation by playing on words and suggesting even that no credence should be given to whatever is being said. Then, the gardener Antonio arrives complaining that his flowerbeds have been destroyed by a man, looking like the page, whom he has seen jumping from the window. At this point, Figaro intervenes to say that it is he who jumped and denies Antonio's hypothesis by reminding him that the page has been sent away to the army. If so, Antonio wishes to return to Figaro a paper which fell out of the pocket of the man who jumped. The count seizes the paper which is nothing else but the officer's commission belonging to Chérubin. In a series of rapid asides, the countess informs Suzanne that the count is holding the officer's commission, which lacks his seal. This information, relayed to Figaro by Suzanne in another series of asides, enables him to argue that Chérubin left the document with him for the count to approve it. According to Jean Meyer, these scenes involving Figaro are to be played slowly to show how much "he stumbles at ever step."[8]

The count resents Figaro's cunning and admits in an aside that he "is at the bottom of everything" (II, 21). Therefore, Almaviva is elated when Marceline arrives claiming her right to marry the servant. He orders that preparations be made forthwith to have the matter examined at a court session over which he will preside. As he denies Bazile's claim to marry Marceline, it is clear that he intends to decide in her favor.

At the conclusion of the act, Figaro is at a further disadvantage when the countess, weary of his previous initiatives, devises her own plan to confound her husband and instructs Suzanne not to reveal it to her fiancé. It is she who will go to the meeting that her husband seeks with the maid.

V   *The Third Act*

Reflecting upon the events, the count is seized with a deep suspicion. Where is Chérubin? Who is the author of the note? Why did Suzanne have to lock herself up in the closet? Who really jumped from the window? Why did the countess show in turn great distress and simulated joy? Above all, did Suzanne reveal the secret of the meeting he so ardently desires? Sounding out Figaro on this point is necessary. If the servant accepts to accompany him to London, where he was appointed an ambassador, it will mean that Suzanne has not spoken. If he refuses, she did speak, for he shows thereby that he seeks to keep his future wife away from his master. Thus, Almaviva first informs Figaro that he will not take him along since he does not know English. The servant replies, in the famous "God-dam tirade,"[9] that knowing the word "God-dam," "the core of the English language" (III, 5), he will get along fine. The count feels reassured. However, Figaro, who realizes that his master is sounding him out, quickly adds that, on the other hand, he is very pleased with his position at the castle. Going to London would force him to leave his wife behind too often. Besides, the hypocrisy of politics does not appeal to him. In this battle of wits, Figaro gains no advantage, for he has now led the count to believe that Suzanne has spoken. Therefore, Almaviva is determined to favor Marceline's claim.

When Suzanne seductively informs the count that she is acceding to his request, he envisions a favorable outcome for Figaro. Indeed, with the dowry she would receive in exchange for the droit du seigneur, he would be able to pay Marceline. However, the possibility of such a happy ending is quickly reversed, as Suzanne thoughtlessly tells her fiancé within the count's earshot: "You have just won your suit" (III, 10). Thus, the count reverts to his original intention to hinder Figaro's marriage. Should the latter find other resources to pay Marceline, Almaviva would ask Antonio to oppose the marriage of his niece to Figaro, a man of unknown parentage.

The episode of the trial is rightly considered a pure fantasy on Beaumarchais's part, since it is extraneous to the main action of the play and, moreover, does not even depict the judicial system of the time. As observed by Félix Gaiffe, it is merely a satire on the numerous trials that wearied Beaumarchais's life from 1770 to 1778.[10] It remains, however, a very amusing interlude. Beaumarchais introduces Don Guzman (an allusion to Goezman) Brid'oison, the stuttering judge who is excessively formalistic and stupid to the point of not understanding Figaro's telling him that he fathered his child. There is also Double-Main ("Double-Hand"), the judge's greedy secretary, who is also the clerk of the court and the ever-yelping usher.

The importance of this court is evidently diminished by the fact that the count retains the sole authority to make a final judgment. Legal minutiae are also mocked when the question arises whether Figaro promised "to pay *and* marry" or "to pay *or* marry" Marceline. As the clerk is unable to read the blotted passage of the document, Bartholo, who defends Marceline, argues for the first version, whereas Figaro maintains that he wrote the second. The litigation is solved by the count whose decision is apparently fair but suited to his own purpose: within the day, Figaro must either pay or marry Marceline.

The servant now tries to escape the verdict by arguing that he cannot enter a marriage without consulting his parents, for whom he has been searching and is about to find. As he mentions a mark imprinted on his arm at birth, Marceline recognizes in him a son she bore of a liaison with Bartholo. This is the recognition scene by which Beaumarchais meant to touch his audiences. Yet, it is also useful from the dramatic point of view for it eliminates at last the count's pretext for hindering his servant's marriage. When Bartholo persists in his refusal to marry Marceline, she chides him and all men who seduce helpless girls. Bartholo's attitude still makes possible Antonio's opposition to the marriage, as Figaro remains without a father. However, Marceline rightfully points out that Figaro can look forward to his future happiness with Suzanne, who is to reach her majority soon and will thus be able to free herself of Antonio's guardianship. The brief misunderstanding which arises when Suzanne sees her fiancé embrace Marceline, whom she still believes to be her rival, is merely meant to introduce to Suzanne Marceline as

Figaro's mother. At the end of the act, Bartholo is almost willing to marry Marceline. In addition to being exempt from paying Marceline, Figaro is enriched by a purse originally given to Suzanne by the countess to pay Marceline. Consequently, the count rightly observes that everything conspires against him.

VI   *The Fourth Act*

Viewing their future happiness, Figaro and Suzanne recapitulate the events and speak of their love. Figaro proclaims love to be a truth powerful enough to defy all others and he seeks of his fiancée a promise of unbounded affection. In his exaltation, he obtains from her a commitment not to go to the meeting still desired by the count. Consequently, the maid informs her mistress that it will not take place. For a moment, the countess is distressed. She asks her maid to help her reconquer her husband by merely inviting him to a meeting to which she herself will go disguised as Suzanne. The bond between the two women is too strong to loosen. Under her mistress' dictation, Suzanne writes to the count that she intends to meet him in the evening under the chestnut trees. The note is sealed with a pin which the count must send back with his reply.

As Bartholo has accepted to marry Marceline, preparations for his wedding party and that of Figaro are under way. Meanwhile, the girls of the town led by Fanchette have come to offer flowers to the countess. In the group is Chérubin disguised as a girl. The countess, who does not recognize him, gives him a kiss meant for the entire group. Chérubin is soon unmasked by Antonio in the presence of the count. Once again, the countess comes to the page's defense by explaining that he is merely playing a game which originated in her room prior to the closet episode. The count's anger toward Chérubin is milder than before, all the more since his promiscuity is revealed by Fanchette. She states that since he usually promises everything to her in exchange for her favors, she would like his consent to marry the page. Almaviva refuses to consider it, preferring to interrogate Figaro once more about the identity of the man who jumped from the window. As Antonio declares that the page admitted jumping, there is no alternative for Figaro but to turn the whole matter into a joke. He explains that both he and the page may have been seized with a jumping fit as were Panurge's sheep. All that remains for the count to do is to dismiss the page, again forbidding him to appear for the rest of the evening. Chérubin says that he could look forward to a dreary future if it were not for the kiss he received from the countess.

The double wedding party is momentarily interrupted by the untimely arrival of Bazile. He claims Marceline's hand according to a previous commitment on her part pending upon her finding a lost son that he is willing to adopt. As the whole matter is long disposed of, Beaumarchais's intention to make Bazile appear utterly ridiculous is evident. However, the altercation between Figaro and Bazile is an amusing scene of verbal acrobatics much practiced by Beaumarchais. Ultimately, Bazile remounces Marceline on his own, as he is horrified by the idea of having a son like Figaro.

Although the detailed indications given by Beaumarchais in the ninth scene have been omitted in Jean Meyer's staging,[11] they are essential insofar as they deal with the remaining intrigue to be solved, namely, the projected meeting between the count and Suzanne. As the maid adjusts the virginal cap she receives from the count during the wedding ceremony, she hands him surreptitiously the invitation to meet her. Figaro witnesses the count's delight and notices that he has pricked his finger with a pin. The servant rightly observes that his master is probably reading a billet-doux. At this point, however, Figaro has no other information about the current events. Upon meeting Fanchette running an errand, he surmises that it is not unrelated to the count's gallant adventure. In her childish naiveté, she readily admits to him that the count has asked her to hand Suzanne a pin and to tell her that it is "the seal for the big chestnut trees" (IV, 14). Jealousy soon fills Figaro's heart, although he has just declared to his mother that he is ready to forgive Suzanne any infidelity. As Marceline advises him not to take a mere suspicion as evidence, he tells her that he will see for himself by going to the meeting place. In an act of feminine solidarity, Marceline plans to inform Suzanne of her son's intention.

VII   *The Fifth Act*

The decor of this eventful last act represents a park of chestnut trees with two pavilions on either side while the stage is dark. Fanchette has come to the park where Chérubin has asked her to meet him. Upon seeing Figaro, she flees into the pavilion at the left. Her joyful nonchalance strongly contrasts with the somber mood of the servant who enters dressed like a conspirer in a cloak and a turned-down hat. As Figaro did at the end of the first act, he has gathered the entire household of the castle of Aguas-Frescas to witness the count caught in the act of seducing his bride. Schérer observes that Figaro has organized here a daring mass action intended to challenge feudal authority, for Bartholo aptly reminds him "that a wise man never meddles in the affairs of great people" (V, 2).[12]

Then Figaro embarks upon his famous monologue which can be divided into three parts. First, he reflects upon his situation. Suzanne is nothing but a deceitful woman whose reluctance to meet the count was a pure sham and who is about to break the pledge she has just made to him. Yet, the count should not think that he can seduce her just because he was privileged to have been born an aristocrat. Secondly, Figaro considers his destiny by giving a detailed account of his past life. A child of unknown parents, he was a jack-of-all-trades having met little success in any of them. Tired of being a veterinary and a barber, he became a playwright. As censorship destroyed him, he set about to write on economics. His ideas on this subject being judged subversive, he was thrown into prison. Upon regaining his freedom, he edited a paper which he called *The Useless Journal*, since it was forbidden to discuss nearly any topic. Such sarcasm caused him to be censored once more and consequently left unemployed. He was a little more successful as a gambler but was hardly allowed to exist by those who proved shrewder than he. He became a barber once more and met a former master whom he helped to get a wife and who now shows his gratitude by trying to seduce his own. Finally, Figaro reflects existentially upon his past, wondering why it has been such and not otherwise. He presents a dialectical self-portrait which encompasses all aspects of his conflicting personality. He ends his monologue by evoking again Suzanne to whom he says, "How you torment me!" (V, 3). As it is explained by Gaiffe, Figaro, in his monologue, thinks through an association of ideas which makes the connection between its three parts psychological rather than logical.[13]

The monologue has long been the subject of conflicting criticism.[14] Sainte-Beuve thought that it turns Figaro into a pedant. For Sarcey it is a dramatic monstrosity which contributes nothing to the main action and unduly delays it. Brunetière, on the other hand, feels that the monologue is as integral a part of the play as Hamlet's. Such a view prevails, for Figaro, through his monologue, raises himself above the usual type of a comic valet.[15]

The lively games of mistaken identity that occupy the remainder of the act restore the comic tension that was suspended by the monologue. The countess enters disguised as Suzanne. The maid, who has been forewarned of Figaro's presence by Marceline and wishes to challenge his trust, has decided to accompany her mistress disguised in the latter's dress. Marceline, who wishes to observe the events, follows Fanchette in the pavilion at the left. While Figaro walks to one end of the stage waiting for the arrival of the count, Suzanne leaves her mistress and walks to the other. As the countess awaits the arrival of the count, she is met by Chérubin who seeks Fanchette. He rightly mistakes the countess for Suzanne and tells her that he will kiss her twenty times for her own sake and a hundred times for her mistress'. He justifies his audacity by explaining that he feels entitled to replace the count with her as she has replaced her mistress with the count. However, the kisses do not reach their destination, for the count arrives suddenly on the scene. This is enough of a reason for Chérubin to flee and seek refuge in the pavilion at the left.

As Figaro wishes to catch Chérubin in the act of seducing the countess disguised as Suzanne, he receives a blow given by the count, who thinks that he has hit the page. With the retreat of Figaro, the count is free to undertake his own seduction as it befits an experienced ladies' man. He tells the countess disguised as Suzanne that he finds her skin soft and smooth, her arm firm and well-rounded, her fingers pretty, graceful, and full of mischief. He says that he seeks pleasure rather than love. On being asked whether he no longer loves his wife, he replies that he does but has become weary of her affection. Pleasurable diversions are necessary, and with a touch of caprice, Suzanne could become "the most provoking mistress" (V, 8). Such pleasure is so priceless to him that he not only hands over to her the dowry but adds to it a diamond. All that is left is to make love, and he entices the disguised countess to accompany him into one of the pavilions. Figaro, who has followed the scene with dismay, steps forward to intervene. Upon seeing him, the count flees as the countess enters into the pavilion at the right.

The stage is now ready for a confrontation between the jealous

Figaro and Suzanne disguised as the countess. He informs her that he is being betrayed by his bride, who has gone off with the count and that he is ready to call for help. As Suzanne, for a moment, fails to disguise her voice, he recognizes her. He masters the joy resulting from his profound relief and proposes a liaison that would duplicate that of the count. For such a suspicious and vindictive Figaro, Suzanne has only blows. At this point, he tells her that he happily accepts them as proof of her love. Unmasked, Suzanne informs him that the count has been courting none other than his own wife, and Figaro must admit that the planning of such a scheme goes far beyond his own ruse.

The count reappears and is about to enter the pavilion at the right in search of the disguised countess when he notices the disguised Suzanne being entertained by Figaro. When Almaviva hears his servant speaking about having jumped from the window, the enigma of the man hidden in the closet becomes clear to him. As the disguised Suzanne flees into the pavilion at the left, the count seizes Figaro and declares him under arrest. At first, the servant affects a simulated fright but soon displays a calmness that exasperates the count. Asked by his master to identify the lady he has just led to the pavilion, Figaro roguishly points to the pavilion at the right and, in turn, asks the count whether it is the one he means. When Almaviva replies that he means the one at the left, Figaro proceeds to identify the lady about whom he says, "I know that a great lord paid her certain attentions, but either because he neglects her, or because I please her better than a more lovable man, today she gave me the preference" (V, 12). Thus, there is no doubt in the count's mind as to the guilt of his wife.

At the door of the pavilion at the left, the count calls upon his wife to come out and admit her infidelity in the presence of the entire household of the castle. Believing that he has seized her, he realizes upon coming out that he holds none other then Chérubin. Ordered by the count to seize the countess, Antonio brings out Fanchette. Bartholo, who has offered to accomplish the mission, does not do much better, as he emerges with Marceline. When Suzanne comes out by herself falling upon her knees and hiding her face with her fan, all assembled fall to their knees and beseech the count to forgive the one they believe to be his wife. As he repeatedly refuses in his anger, the disguised countess emerges from the pavilion at the right and joins the others in falling on her knees. Thereupon, the count looks at both Suzanne and the countess, realizes their scheme, and admits, "I tried to deceive them, and they have played with me like a child" (V, 19). As for Figaro, he receives from the countess the dowry and the diamond.

The joyous vaudeville which closes the play is composed of ten couplets. In the first, Bazile praises Figaro who has gained a triple dowry and a splendid wife, and who harbors no jealousy toward the count or the page. In the second couplet, Suzanne decries the unjust domination of man over woman, and in the ninth, she sings of the gaiety of the play which also teaches a moral lesson. Figaro mocks a jealous husband in the third, insults Bartholo in the sixth and, in the seventh, extols wit that can overshadow inequality of birth. In the fourth, the countess praises the faithful wife, while, in the fifth, the count is more daring in singing of the one who can "play a merry game." In the sixth, Marceline sings of him who can only be sure of being the son of his mother, while the rest is love's secret. In the eighth, Chérubin compares an audience to women. He says that one always seeks to please the former in the same way one cannot resist the latter. In the final couplet, Brid'oison says that the play just presented is a true image of life, where, despite justified complaints, everything ends in a song.

VIII *The Characters*

Count Almaviva represents a typical eighteenth-century nobleman who likes to indulge in amorous adventures. However, self-esteem is a supreme aspect of his character. Therefore, he cannot bear that Suzanne opposes his advances or that his wife may be unfaithful to him. His eagerness to seduce one and watch the movements of the other turns him into a comic character, for he becomes the victim of both who succeed in outwitting him. Yet, Beaumarchais, who admired aristocracy, recommended that the role of the count "should be played with nobility." Indeed, as a lord and master, Almaviva exercises an unequivocal authority that constantly threatens the projects of those who try to foil his intentions. At the end of the play, he gracefully accepts his defeat.

Figaro is the count's most direct opponent. To keep Suzanne away from his master, he must exploit all the resources of his wit. He does so in forcing the count to abolish, officially at least, the droit du seigneur, in inventing the infidelity of the countess, in retaining

Chérubin at the castle, and in organizing two mass movements that challenge the authority of the count. In view of his position, there cannot be more concrete actions for him to undertake. In fact, he loses control of the intrigue, which is taken over by the countess when she decides to substitute herself for Suzanne. Thanks to his ruse and wit, he will always disentangle himself from embarrassing situations, and, rightfully perhaps, does the count look upon his actions with suspicion. Figaro becomes even somewhat ridiculous when, despite his assertions to the contrary, he yields to jealousy over Suzanne's supposed infidelity. Such weakness is largely compensated by his ability to transform this setback into a moment of profound introspection and his determination to stand up for his rights. At the end of the play, when he finds himself married to Suzanne, untouched by the count, and in possession of three dowries, it is indeed the work of fate as he himself admits.

As an abandoned wife, the countess is a moving character. She suffers with a dignity that befits her noble rank. Her sensitivity and emotional dismay appear at their best in the "closet episode." When it ends happily at the expense of the count, it is no wonder that he sees in her a marvelous actress, since she was truly exposing her innermost self. Her affection for Chérubin is the natural response of a heart that intensely seeks the warmth of love. The nature of Chérubin's feelings are so akin to hers that she only renounces him at the very end of the play. Yet, she does not accept her fate passively. To regain her husband is her major concern, and, to this end, she takes a carefully planned initiative which is resourceful enough to sustain the action of the last three acts.

Suzanne is not only the lady in waiting of the countess but also her confidante. She reveals to her mistress the frivolous intentions of the count thereby enabling her to act. Perfect harmony exists between the two women so that when this harmony is momentarily threatened by Suzanne's hesitation to cooperate with the countess' project, they soon regret having antagonized each other. Knowing that Chérubin's gallantry is a pleasant diversion for her mistress, she encourages it tacitly. Her seductive capriciousness frustrates the count's desires when she eludes his pursuit but fills his heart with joy when she accepts to meet him. She is intent on becoming a faithful wife to Figaro and sternly frowns upon any suspicion he may have about her sincerity.

For Benedetto Croce, the character of Chérubin is a poetic masterpiece since he represents "the heightened amorous temperament, for which the highest ideal and vital principle are the love of love."[16] Although such a view is accurate, it remains idealistic and does not account for the dramatic function of Chérubin. The page is depicted as a youth who discovers love as shown by his boldness toward any woman. Because of the countess' social position, his feelings toward her take the form of a passionate respect, which is shown in the romance he sings for her and his persistence in retaining the ribbon he stole from her. Chérubin also symbolizes the sensuality that pervades the play, as he delights in roaming around women's quarters and toying with their clothes. He repeatedly finds himself in the count's way thereby reminding him of his frivolity, and, in a sense, he is the count's rival as he, too, pursues the countess, Suzanne, and Fanchette. As a junior officer, Chérubin is conscious of his honor, and he stands ready to challenge the count, who teases him about the slap he believes to have given to him in the park of the chestnut trees.

Marceline is chiefly concerned with finding a husband and defending women's rights. In this respect, she has rightly been described as an "overeager" female to the point of being comic.[17] Until she recognizes Figaro as her son, she constitutes a strong obstacle to his marriage. As Suzanne's future mother-in-law, she warns her of Figaro's unfounded jealousy.

At first, Bartholo's role consists in defending Marceline's claim to marry Figaro. When this issue is eliminated, he himself marries her, thus solving her matrimonial problem as well as that of Figaro's legitimacy. As Figaro's father, he wisely reminds him to be careful in opposing a nobleman such as Almaviva.

Bazile loses the count's confidence when he fails to check the veracity of the note concerning the countess' infidelity. From this moment on, he is merely ridiculous as he utters banal proverbs and plays insipid music.

Brid'oison's legal authority is doubtful, as he insists on respecting formalities and considering as final decisions that are made by the count. Yet, despite his stupidity, he rightly observes in the course of the last act that the events of this "mad day" are all too confusing, and the play closes on a truthful observation made by him.

Antonio, the tipsy gardener, is lucid enough to force Figaro and

Chérubin into embarrassing situations or to oppose the marriage of his niece Suzanne to the illegitimate Figaro. The naiveté of his daughter Fanchette is to be viewed as a precocious sensuality. She has learned much in the company of Chérubin and never refuses that of the count. It is thanks to her candid revelations that Figaro becomes aware of the projected meeting between the count and Suzanne.

Grippe-Soleil and Pédrille are overzealous servants of the count. By forbidding the first to set up the fireworks under the chestnut trees, the count saves his meeting place from a potential fire. In obeying the count's orders, the second does not understand that arresting Figaro is far more important than reporting on his vain search for Chérubin.

IX *Originality and Significance*

Beaumarchais sacrifices verisimilitude again in the *Mariage de Figaro*, in which many questions remain unanswered. Why does Figaro allow himself to be outwitted by other characters and by Fate? What precise relationship existed formerly between Marceline and Figaro? Why is she so eager to marry the one who turns out to be her son? Why does not Suzanne save her bridegroom from an unfavorable verdict by paying Marceline earlier with the dowry offered by the countess? What does Figaro really gain by suddenly changing his mind about the count's proposal to go to London? Why does Almaviva accept Suzanne's proposal to meet him when he has serious reasons to mistrust her? Why does not Suzanne find a way to inform Figaro that she is substituting herself for her mistress?

Rigorous logic would undoubtedly have damaged the vivaciousness that results from Beaumarchais's own way of connecting and presenting the events. In constructing his complex intrigue, the author reaches the heights of comic imagination. Until the end of the play, one constantly wonders whether the advantage lies with Figaro or the count. Chérubin's reappearances constitute an example of a comic situation based on repetition. Peripeteia multiply themselves with unusual rapidity in the "armchair" or "closet" episodes. In the last act, the accumulation of unexpected occurrences is a resourceful comic device amid disguises, hiding-places, and darkness. An atmosphere of subtle voluptuousness hovers over the play where pins, ribbons, virginal togas, and feminine clothes become exquisite symbols of sensuality. When the stream of joy is occasionally suspended, it is replaced by touching scenes. Such are the episodes of Chérubin singing his romance before the countess or even that of Marceline finding her lost child.

In the *Mariage de Figaro,* the comic style largely consists of Beaumarchais's efforts to have each of his characters speak his own language. Its variety ranges from Figaro's unequaled verve to Grippe-Soleil's mispronounced words. Verbal exchanges and lively dialogues are frequent occasions for laughter in the trial scene, in meetings between Figaro and the count, or in those between Figaro and Bazile. Style becomes even delightfully precious when Figaro and Suzanne find the time to speak of their love. Even Figaro's monologue is a rare example of volubility, especially when one keeps in mind the fact that its previous versions were much longer. Although many episodes are unessential to the main action, they show Beaumarchais's ability to juggle with words and invent repartee.

Throughout the play, Figaro does not lose any opportunity to criticize aristocrats, and, in the very last scene, he has some harsh words for their manner of dispensing justice. Eighteenth-century audiences did not fail to see the far-reaching social and political implications of the *Mariage* amid its joyfulness. Most representative of them is the Baronne d'Oberkirch, who was angry with herself for having been amused by it. She writes: ". . . nobility showed a great want of tact in applauding it, which was nothing less than giving themselves a slap in the face. They laughed at their own expense, and what was worse they made others laugh too. They will repent it yet. . . ."[18] Judging the work in retrospect, Napoleon thought that it portrayed "the Revolution in action." Even today Beaumarchais's play is viewed as a vivid illustration of the class struggle.[19]

Critics have carefully weighed the theory of Beaumarchais as a revolutionary, and most of them discard it. Beaumarchais never meant to advocate the overthrow of the monarchy and its institutions. In his preface to the play, he specifically reasserted his respect for nobility by quoting from his own *mémoires* against La Blache, where he declares that "the right of birth should be the least contested of all." In fact, Beaumarchais was himself a victim of the evils of the Revolution, having seen the magnificent house he had built opposite the Bastille repeatedly searched and eventually devastated, having barely escaped the guillotine, and having lived in exile as an émigré. In his comedy, Beaumarchais meant to attack merely excesses and abuses. Insofar as it claims the rights of the illegitimate child, of women, and of the individual to enjoy his freedom and to obtain a fair trial, it remains eternally universal.

The uniqueness of the *Mariage de Figaro* lies much in the profound relationship that exists between the work and the life of its author. Almaviva's frivolity is one that Beaumarchais himself pursued. The portrayal of feminine characters shows an insight into a woman's heart by someone who both loved women and was loved by them. There is much of the young Caron in the daring mischievousness of Chérubin. Figaro represents the author in his numerous enterprises and struggles. As for the episodes of the play that do not necessarily relate to the central plot, they remain echoes of authentic events. Yet, all these characters and situations are raised to the level of a perfected comic art which gives the play its blustering rhythm. Beaumarchais should not be taken seriously when he states in his preface that the play teaches a moral lesson. In asserting this, he merely uses an old device to transmit to posterity a sublime masterpiece.

CHAPTER 6

Conclusion

THE relationship between an author and his work is a frequent
subject for literary controversy. In the case of Beaumarchais, it
is impossible to separate one from the other, for many of his writings
grew out of his numerous adventures, trials, and tribulations. The
ambitious young watchmaker must already defend in a well-ordered
mémoire the originality of his inventions. In his eagerness to be convincing, the accuser of Goezman and La Blache must enliven the dry
legality of his arguments with irony and wit. The sensitive man
transforms the case of a mistreated wife into a *cause célèbre*. The
secret agent knows the art of arousing suspense when reporting on
his missions, becomes an expert at political intrigue, and succeeds in
proving that he is indispensable. The businessman easily shows that
his enterprises are motivated by reasons that go beyond self-interest.

As an author of mémoires, Beaumarchais is not a mere defendant.
He is a skillful writer who organizes his ideas, selects his language,
evokes antiquity, imitates Rabelais, and pleads with eloquence. He
describes his confrontations with Madame Goezman in sketches that
are deemed amusing enough to be acted out at the court of Louis
XV. He ridicules his enemies in biting caricatures, and his en-
counters with Clavijo inspire Goethe and other playwrights. While
the later mémoires are less polished, they remain eloquent pleas in
which Beaumarchais occasionally presents interesting portraits and
vivid tableaux.

The genre larmoyant, which depicts bourgeois life, is a literary
fashion of the eighteenth century. With pretensions to writing plays,
Beaumarchais tries his hand at dramas. Inspired by Diderot, his
Essai sur le genre dramatique sérieux is a keen defense of the drama
and presents some original ideas on the technique of the theater.
However, the dramas themselves, *Eugénie* and *Les Deux Amis*,
depict highly unrealistic situations, which Beaumarchais often com-

plicates in order to make them more consistent. The same defects reappear in the sentimental episodes of *Le Mariage de Figaro* and in *La Mère coupable*, a sequel to the two comedies which is again a drama. Bourgeois realism is not a very fertile subject for the theater. Yet, eighteenth-century audiences delighted in it for it afforded them the opportunity to be moved and shed tears. In this respect, Beaumarchais has been successful for his dramas contain many touching scenes.

While Beaumarchais's *Parades* were written for specific occasions and represent a genre which is a fashion of the times, they must be considered as an introduction to his comedies. Deceiving a more artful deceiver is already the subject of those sketches, which show that Beaumarchais's conception of comedy is based on psychological insight. Such is also the underlying theme of the comedies. Through the carefully worked out succession of ingenious schemes aimed at overcoming Bartholo's suspicion, *Le Barbier de Séville* is a highly amusing comedy of characters and situations. *Le Mariage de Figaro* is a combination of several intrigues. In a whirlwind of gaiety, the characters disguise themselves, run on and off the stage, go in and out of hiding-places. Moreover, the *Mariage* is raised to the level of a subtle satire of characters and mores. The comic art of both comedies is heightened by a quick-witted language.

Beaumarchais is also an innovator as a man of the theater. The opposition between character and situation as set forth in the *Essai* is a fertile device for creating tension both in drama and comedy. *Eugénie* brings to the stage the daring jeux d'entr'actes that were to make the play more cohesive. Beaumarchais is a scrupulous stage director who describes with precision the psychological state of his characters and gives detailed indications concerning decor, clothing, staging, and lighting. In the comedies, he has devised the succession of péripéties-éclairs, which generate peals of laughter. He is concerned with the role of music in the theater, and, through his opera *Tarare*, he proposes that it should be a subdued auxiliary of the dramatic poem. Finally, he informs us of his own conception of dramatic technique in his preface to the *Mariage:* "When my subject seizes me, I call out all my characters and place them in a situation. . . . What they will say, I know not at all; it's what they will do that concerns me. Then, when they are fully come to life, I write under their rapid dictation. . . ."

Critics have often searched for the origin of the name Figaro. When one considers the stature of such a lasting creation, it is immaterial to know whether it is derived from *fils Caron* or from the expression *faire la figue,* which means to laugh at the world. Surely, the servant as a comic character is known since Molière. Throughout the theater of the eighteenth century, he becomes so ambitious that he represents a real challenge to his master. Figaro may seem the culmination of such an evolution. Yet, to judge him in such a perspective alone is insufficient, for his role goes beyond the realm of mere laughter. He bears a profound resemblance to his creator as he reveals himself from the outset as a man for all seasons. His gaiety surely recalls that of his literary ancestor Panurge, but it also shows an optimistic attitude toward a life that brought him many misfortunes. As much as his boasting, quibbling, and tricking amuse us, he appears for a moment suspicious in our eyes. However, one soon realizes that his behavior is dictated by a fear of becoming the victim of unscrupulous men of power. Figaro is neither wicked nor dishonest, nor does he intend to upset the established order. He is a man of his times, sensitive but aware of his rights. His cheerfulness is almost inexhaustible, but, in moments of crisis, he is serious and proud. As he ages, he proves to be a faithful servant.

Notes and References

Chapter One

1. *Correspondance,* ed. Brian N. Morton (Paris: Nizet, 1969), I, 6.
2. Eugène Lintilhac, *Beaumarchais et ses oeuvres* (Paris: Hachette, 1887), p. 374.
3. *Oeuvres complètes* (Paris: Ledentu, 1837), p. 280. Except for all plays and unless otherwise indicated, all references to the works of Beaumarchais appearing henceforth in parentheses will be to this edition.
4. See Bernard Fay, *Beaumarchais ou les fredaines de Figaro* (Paris: Librairie Académique Perrin, 1971), p. 129.
5. *Beaumarchais* (Paris: Hatier, 1962), p. 24.
6. *Correspondance,* I, 125-30.
7. The terms *franc* or *livre* are equivalent in the eighteenth century. They represent approximately the value of the present dollar. See Pomeau, p. 13, n. 1.
8. *Correspondance,* II, 35.
9. *Ibid.,* 34.
10. *Beaumarchais et son temps* (Paris: Lévy, 1856), I, 312.
11. See *Beaumarchais,* p. 85.
12. Linthilhac, p. 389.
13. *Correspondance,* II, 56.
14. *Ibid.,* p. 68.
15. *Ibid.,* p. 72.
16. *Ibid.,* p. 116
17. See *Beaumarchais et ses oeuvres,* p. 65.
18. See *Beaumarchais,* p. 57.
19. Quoted by Loménie, I, 416.
20. *Ibid.,* 433-34.
21. *Correspondance,* II, 156.
22. *Ibid.,* 142, n. 3.
23. See *Beaumarchais,* p. 237.
24. *Correspondance,* II, 244.
25. Quoted by Loménie, II, 149.
26. *Ibid.,* p. 196.
27. Quoted by Lintilhac, p. 123.
28. See *Beaumarchais et son temps,* II, p. 87.

29. According to Pomeau, p. 66, there is nothing to prove that Catherine II ever had such an intention.

30. Quoted by Loménie, II, 222.

Chapter Two

1. *Beaumarchais et ses oeuvres*, pp. 144-47.

2. "The literary technique of the first two *Mémoires* of Beaumarchais against Goezman," *Studies on Voltaire and the Eighteenth Century* 47 (1966), 202.

3. Quoted by Cynthia Cox, *The Real Figaro: The Extraordinary Life of Caron de Beaumarchais* (London: Longmans, 1962), p. 60.

4. *Correspondance*, ed. Theodore Besterman (Genève, 1953-65), LXXXVII, 83.

5. See Lintilhac, p. 46, n. 3.

6. *Correspondance*, XC, 90.

7. Quoted by P. Ph. Gudin de la Brenellerie, *Histoire de Beaumarchais*, ed. Maurice Tourneux (Paris: Plon, 1888), p. 102.

8. Quoted by Loménie, I, 348.

9. *Beaumarchais et ses oeuvres*, p. 155.

10. *Causeries du Lundi* (Paris: Garnier, n.d.), VI, 252.

11. *Beaumarchais* (Paris, 1897), p. 153.

12. "La Dernière Aventure de Beaumarchais: L'Affaire des fusils de Hollande," *Archives des Lettres Modernes*, no. 111 (Paris: Minard, 1970), pp. 40-54.

13. On this subject, see my article "Du Côté de Beaumarchais," *Les Nouveaux Cahiers*, no. 24 (Printemps, 1971), pp. 32-34.

Chapter Three

1. Brian N. Morton, "Beaumarchais' first play *Eugénie*," *Romanic Review* 57 (1966), 81-87.

2. *La Dramaturgie de Beaumarchais* (Paris: Nizet, 1954), pp. 130, 141.

3. See Anthony R. Pugh, "Beaumarchais, the 'drame bourgeois' and the pièce bien faite,'" *Modern Language Review* 61 (1966), 416.

4. *La Dramaturgie de Beaumarchais*, p. 136.

5. "Beaumarchais, the 'drame bourgeois,'" pp. 417-18.

6. *Beaumarchais et son temps*, II, 418.

7. *La Dramaturgie de Beaumarchais*, pp. 121-29.

8. "A M. Martineau," *Théâtre Complet*, ed. Maurice Allem et Paul-

Courant, Bibliothèque de la Pléiade (Paris: Gallimard, 1957), p. 704.

9. *Histoire de Beaumarchais*, p. 407.

10. *Beaumarchais*, p. 190.

11. "A M. Martineau," p. 702.

Chapter Four

1. *La Dramaturgie de Beaumarchais*, p. 188.

2. Beaumarchais, *Théâtre complet*, Bibliothèque de la Pléiade, p. 821.

3. "Les Parades de Beaumarchais," *L'Information Littéraire*, no. 3 (1951), pp. 43-50.

4. *Beaumarchais et ses oeuvres*, pp. 219-21.

5. See *La Dramaturgie de Beaumarchais*, p. 136.

6. "*Le Barbier de Séville* et la critique," *French Studies* XVI (1962), 342-44. Arnould seems less categorical in his edition of *Le Mariage de Figaro* (Oxford: Blackwell, 1968), p. xviii, where he writes that the *Barbier* finds "perhaps" its origin in a "parade."

7. *Beaumarchais nel suo e nel nostro tempo: Le Barbier de Séville* (Roma: Edizioni dell' Ateneo, 1964), pp. 315-16.

8. *La Dramaturgie de Beaumarchais* (Paris: Nizet, 1967), p. 7.

9. *Le Barbier de Séville*, ed. E.J. Arnould (Oxford: Blackwell, 1963), p. 107, n. 70.

10. Gudin de la Brenellerie, *Histoire de Beaumarchais*, pp. 78-79.

11. *Beaumarchais et ses oeuvres*, pp. 213-57.

12. For a description, chronology, and reproduction of the various manuscripts of the *Barbier*, see E.J. Arnould, *La Génèse du Barbier de Séville* (Dublin: Dublin Univ. Press & Paris: Minard, 1965).

13. *La Dramaturgie de Beaumarchais*, pp. 149-54.

14. Enzo Giudici, *Beaumarchais*, pp. 735-55, examines some of Figaro's faults. We have chosen to follow the approach which considers him a congenial character.

Chapter Five

1. On the background of this question see Jacques Seebacher, "Autour de 'Figaro': Beaumarchais, la famille de Choiseul et le financier Clavière," *Revue de l'Histoire Littéraire de la France* 62 (1962), 199-228.

2. Guy Michaud, "L'intrigue at les ressorts du comique dans *Le Mariage de Figaro*," *L'Oeuvre et ses techniques* (Paris: Nizet, 1957), p. 250.

3. *La Dramaturgie de Beaumarchais*, pp. 176-77.

4. Michaud, "L'intrigue," p. 252.

5. Beaumarchais, *Le Mariage de Figaro*, ed. Jean Meyer, (Paris: Editions du Seuil, 1953), p. 11.

6. Schérer explains the closet episode by stressing the importance of the five dramatic locations which are respectively the bedroom, the closet, the window, the back door, and the alcove. See *Le Mariage de Figaro*, ed. Jacques Schérer (Paris: SEDES, 1966), pp. 156-61.

7. Claude Vincenot points out that the comic situation here arises from the fact that a truth (the real presence of Suzanne) results from the two successive lies uttered by the countess (the first concerning the real presence of Chérubin, the second concerning the real presence of Suzanne). For more applications of this principle throughout the play, see his article "Mensonge, erreur et vérité dans *Le Mariage de Figaro*," *Revue des Sciences Humaines*, Fascicule no. 134 (Avril-Juin, 1969), 219-27.

8. *Le Mariage de Figaro*, p. 12.

9. This tirade was originally written for the five-act version of the *Barbier*.

10. *Le Mariage de Figaro* (Paris: Centre de Documentation Universitaire, 1964), pp. 147-48.

11. *Le Mariage de Figaro*, p. 231.

12. *Le Mariage de Figaro*, p. 351.

13. *Le Mariage de Figaro*, p. 166.

14. *Ibid.*, p. 165.

15. Roger Pons, "Le Monologue de Figaro" *L'Information Littéraire*, no. 3 (1951), 118-22.

16. "Cherubino and the Countess," *Philosophy, Poetry, History: An Anthology of Essays* (London: Oxford Univ. Press, 1966), p. 900.

17. See J. B. Ratermanis & W. R. Irwin, *The Comic Style of Beaumarchais* (Seattle: Washington Univ. Press, 1961), p. 54.

18. Quoted by Cynthia Cox, *The Real Figaro*, pp. 143-44.

19. See *Le Mariage de Figaro*, ed. Annie Ubersfeld (Paris: Editions Sociales, 1966), pp. 24-59.

Selected Bibliography

PRIMARY SOURCES

1. Some Important Editions:

Oeuvres complètes. Ed. by P. Ph. Gudin de la Brenellerie.
   7 Vols. Paris: Collin, 1809.
Oeuvres complètes. Ed. by M. Saint-Marc Girardin.
   Paris: Ledentu, 1837.
Oeuvres complètes. Ed. by Louis Moland. Paris: Garnier, 1874.
Oeuvres complètes. Ed. by E. Fournier. Paris: Laplace, Sanchez & Cie,
   1876. This edition publishes for the first time an incomplete version of
   the *Parades.*
Théâtre complet de Beaumarchais. Ed. by G. d'Heylli and F. de Marescot. 4
   Vols. Paris: Académie des Bibliophiles, 1869–1871. An informative
   critical edition but incomplete as to the variants and original
   manuscripts.
Théâtre complet de Beaumarchais. Ed. by R. d'Hermies. Paris: Magnard,
   1952. Presents the complete text of all dramatic works.
Théâtre complet. Ed. by Maurice Allem and Paul-Courant. Paris: Gallimard
   (Bibliothèque de la Pléiade), 1957. Presents the complete text of all
   dramatic works, the correspondence relating to all plays and variants
   based on a partial use of manuscripts only. Includes useful introduc-
   tions and notes.
Le Barbier de Séville. Ed. by E. J. Arnould. Oxford: Blackwell, 1963.
   Includes a useful introduction which discusses the genesis and
   originality of the play. The footnotes are very informative.
Le Mariage de Figaro. Ed. by Jean Meyer. Paris: Editions du Seuil, 1953.
   Gives directions concerning the stage production of the play. Incisive
   comments are presented in an introduction.
Le Mariage de Figaro. Ed. by Annie Ubersfeld. Paris: Editions Sociales,
   1957. The introduction views the play as an illustration of the class
   struggle which opposes master and slaves in a Marxist context.
Le Mariage de Figaro. Ed. by Jacques Schérer. Paris: Société d'Edition et
   d'Enseignement Supérieur, 1966. The commentary or "analyse
   dramaturgique" which accompanies the text is a brilliant elucidation
   which hardly leaves anything unexplained.

Le Mariage de Figaro. Ed. by J. B. Ratermanis. *Studies on Voltaire and the Eighteenth Century* no. 63. Genève, 1968. Presents the three known manuscripts of the *Mariage* thus showing the various transformations of the play. The notes are very informative.

Correspondance. Ed. by Brian N. Morton. 3 Vols. published to date. Paris: Nizet, 1969. Gathers Beaumarchais's essential letters and includes those written to him. The notes and explanations are informative. A very useful edition and long-awaited enterprise in view of the extreme dispersion of the correspondence to this date.

Notes et Réflexions. Ed. by Gérard Bauer. Paris: Hachette, 1961. Presents interesting musings of Beaumarchais some of which had remained unpublished.

2. Some Translations:

The Barber of Seville, The Marriage of Figaro. Trans. by John Wood. Penguin Books, 1964.

The Barber of Seville. Ed. and trans. by Brobury Pearce Ellis. New York: Appleton-Century-Crofts, 1966.

The Marriage of Figaro. Ed. and trans. by Brobury Pearce Ellis. New York: Appleton-Century-Crofts, 1966.

SECONDARY SOURCES

1. Bibliographies:

CABEEN, DAVID C. *A Critical Bibliography of French Literature, Volume IV: The Eighteenth Century.* Ed. by George R. Havens and Donald F. Bond. Syracuse: Syracuse Univ. Press, 1951. Contains selected items accompanied by judicious comments.

    A Critical Bibliography of French Literature, Volume IV, Supplement: The Eighteenth Century. Ed. by Richard A. Brooks. Syracuse: Syracuse Univ. Press, 1968. Updates the preceding volume following the same method. Remains selective. Both volumes should be used with other existing bibliographies.

CIORANESCU, ALEXANDRE. *Bibliographie de la littérature française du dix-huitième siècle.* 3 Vols. Paris: CNRS, 1969. Under the "Beaumarchais" listing gives a methodical classification of all editions and publications concerning the various aspects of the life and works of Beaumarchais. Slight inaccuracies.

CORDIER, HENRI. *Bibliographie des oeuvres de Beaumarchais.* Paris: Quantin, 1883. Lists all editions of Beaumarchais' writings as well as parodies, translations, and adaptations of his plays published to that date.

KLAPP, OTTO. *Bibliographie d'histoire littéraire française.* Frankfurt: Klostermann, 1956 to date. Gives very complete and accurate listings of editions and critical studies that appear yearly.

2. Biographies:

COX, CYNTHIA. *The Real Figaro: The Extraordinary Career of Caron de Beaumarchais.* London: Longmans, 1962. Well documented and well written.

FAY, BERNARD. *Beaumarchais ou les fredaines de Figaro.* Paris: Librairie Académique Perrin, 1971. Curiously centers Beaumarchais's life around the theme of the woman. Informative but somewhat verbose.

GUDIN DE LA BRENELLERIE, P. PH., *Histoire de Beaumarchais.* Ed. by Maurice Tourneux. Paris: Plon, 1888. Overly favorable and obviously partial as the author was Beaumarchais's secretary and best friend.

LEMAITRE, GEORGES. *Beaumarchais.* New York: Knopf, 1949. Based on standard information and somewhat too favorable. Makes pleasant reading.

RICHARD, PIERRE. *La Vie privée de Beaumarchais.* Paris: Hachette, 1951. Very precise and informative but emphasizes the individual rather than the man of his times.

3. Critical Studies:

ARNOULD, EMILE JULES. *"Le Barbier de Séville* et la critique."* French Studies* 16 (1962), 334–47. Reassesses the chronology of the *Barbier* and challenges Lintilhac, who holds that the play was originally a "parade."

————, *La Génèse du Barbier de Séville.* Dublin: Dublin Univ. Press and Paris: Minard, 1965. The most exhaustive critical edition of the play. Reproduces the three known manuscripts and variants and contains a very detailed introduction and useful comments on the *Lettre modérée* and *Compliment de clôture.*

BEAUMARCHAIS, JEAN-PIERRE DE, "Beaumarchais devant la critique." *L'Information Littéraire,* no. 2 (1973), 55–63. Reviews cursorily the most recent biographical and critical studies.

GAIFFE, FÉLIX. *Le Mariage de Figaro.* Paris: Centre de Documentation Universitaire, 1964. Studies the important scenes of each act. Contains a very detailed introduction which evaluates the play. Should be supplemented, however, by Jacques Schérer's "analyse dramaturgique."

————. *Le Mariage de Figaro.* Paris: Nizet, 1956. A historical study concerning the composition, performance, criticism, and influence of the play.

GIUDICI, ENZO. *Beaumarchais, nel suo e nel nostro tempo: Le Barbier de Séville*. Roma: Edizioni dell' Ateneo, 1964. A very exhaustive study of all aspects of the play considered as a masterpiece on a par with the *Mariage*. Views Figaro with suspicion.

HALLAYS, ANDRÉ. *Beaumarchais*. Paris: Hachette, 1897. Very clear and objective. Emphasizes Beaumarchais's personality rather than his works.

HAMPTON, JOHN. "The literary technique of the first two 'mémoires' of Beaumarchais against Goezman." *Studies on Voltaire and the Eighteenth Century*, no. 47 (1966), 177–205. Points to the unintentional use of literary devices in what was meant to be mere legal pleas.

JOHNSON, MARGARET LEAH. *Beaumarchais and his opponents*. Richmond, Va.: Wipppel and Shepperson, 1936. Examines Beaumarchais's writings concerning his trials in the light of the pamphlets written by his opponents. Not a literary study.

KITE, ELIZABETH S. *Beaumarchais and the War of American Independence*. 2 Vols. Boston: Badger, 1918. Mostly a biographical work. Only chapters 16–22 deal with Beaumarchais's role in the war.

LINTILHAC, EUGENE FRANCOIS. *Beaumarchais et ses oeuvres*. Paris: Hachette, 1887. Basic study supported by an abundant scholarly documentation which makes the reading somewhat difficult at times. Contains supplementary information on Beaumarchais' life. Although controversial at times, the commentary remains generally sound.

LOMENIÉ, LOUIS DE. *Beaumarchais et son temps*. 2 Vols. Paris: Michel Lévy, 1858. Basic biography showing Beaumarchais in the midst of eighteenth-century society. Cursory but sound evaluation of the works.
_____. *Beaumarchais and his times*. Trans. by Henry S. Edwards. New York: Harper and Brothers, 1857.

MICHAUD, GUY. "L'intrigue et les ressorts du comique dans *Le Mariage de Figaro*." *L'Oeuvre et ses techniques*. Paris: Nizet, 1957, 245–59. Penetrating insight into the structure of the play stressing the conflict of interests as they appear in the various intrigues.

POMEAU, RENÉ. *Beaumarchais*. Paris: Hatier, 1962. Clear, concise, and thorough study of the author and his work.

PONS, ROGER. "Le Monologue de Figaro." *L'Information Littéraire*, no. 3 (1951), 118–22. A detailed literary analysis.

PROSCHWITZ, GUNNAR VON. *Introduction à l'étude du vocabulaire de Beaumarchais*. Stockholm: Almrist and Wiksell and Paris: Nizet, 1956. Interesting study of neologisms introduced by Beaumarchais in the fields of literature, politics, and fashion of the times.

PUGH, ANTHONY. "Beaumarchais, the 'drame bourgeois' and the 'pièce bien faite.' " *Modern Language Review* 61 (1966), 416–21. Suggests that Beaumarchais masters the art of building a plot throughout his plays.

RATERMANIS, J. B., and IRWIN, W. R. *The Comic Style of Beaumarchais*. Seattle: Univ. of Washington Press, 1961. Mainly an analysis of the comedies supported by an eclectic study of their style and comic theory.

SCHÉRER, JACQUES. *La Dramaturgie de Beaumarchais*. Paris: Nizet, 1954. Views Beaumarchais's theater as a unity and presents a penetrating analysis of his dramatic technique.

————. "Les Parades de Beaumarchais." *L'Information Littéraire*, no. 2 (1951), 43–50. A comprehensive analysis of the *Parades* which stresses their dramatic value.

VAN TIEGHEM, PHILIPPE. *Beaumarchais par lui-même*. Paris: Editions du Seuil, 1960. Shows that Beaumarchais lives up to the sentimental, philosophic, and pragmatic demands of his times. Should be read as a supplement to already acquired knowledge on Beaumarchais.

VIER, JACQUES. "Beaumarchais." *Histoire de la littérature française du dix-huitième siècle*. Paris: Armand Colin, 1970. Vol. II, pp. 212–68. An interesting reevaluation with original comments on the comedies and *La Mère coupable*.

INDEX

DATE DUE
